TAKING
ON THE MEN

This book is dedicated to two couples, not related to me, who loved and cherished me when I needed it most: John and Angela Pearce and Geoff and Gill Whitfield. Sadly both the Reverend John Pearce and the Reverend Geoffrey Whitfield passed away during the preparation of this book.

TAKING
ON THE MEN

The First Women
Parliamentary Candidates 1918

David Hallam

BREWIN BOOKS

Published in 2018 by Brewin Books

Brewin Books
56 Alcester Road,
Studley,
Warwickshire,
B80 7LG
www.brewinbooks.com

A CIP catalogue record for this book is available
from the British Library.

ISBN: 978-1-85858-592-5

Printed and bound in Great Britain
by Page Bros Ltd.

Contents

Acknowledgements

THIS book is based on a dissertation submitted as part of the fascinating and challenging West Midlands History Master of Arts course run for the University of Birmingham by Dr Malcolm Dick and Dr Matt Cole, both of whom have been a tremendous encouragement, especially Matt Cole in the final weeks of preparation.

Many, many others have helped me with this work. My interest in the subject of electoral behaviour goes back to the 1959 General Election when I undertook my first leaflet distribution and attended my first election meeting. Many of those I met on that journey are now dead, but have greatly contributed to my understanding of the political process.

I would like to thank the staff of the various archives and local studies centres I consulted: Dudley, Sandwell, Birmingham, the Cadbury Research Centre, the TUC archive, the Women's Reading Room at the London School of Economics, and the Museum of London. These are mentioned in detail in my section on sources.

Adam Carey, an old friend, provided valuable assistance in creating a map charting the three constituencies, something that was not available from any other source. It was very useful to speak to several women who were former Parliamentary candidates, one of whom kindly commented on an early version of the paper. Ginny Hartley gave genealogical help and also commented on the final copy. Members of my family undertook detailed reviews and proofreading including my wife Claire and sister Wendy. Michael Willis and my son Owen, both historians, were particularly helpful in formulating my ideas. Steve Coxon did a final proofread and Nicky Cure created a brilliant front cover. I am very grateful to Preet Gill, Britain's first women Sikh Member of Parliament, for writing the foreword.

Jeremy Corbyn MP read an early version of the book and encouraged me to publish it. John Spellar MP kindly helped with the launch. My publisher Brewin Books have been encouraging throughout and they do much to support local history in the West Midlands.

My thanks to all, but errors, omissions and opinions remain my responsibility.

David Hallam
November 2018

Figure 1: Political Map of West Midlands following the 1918 Representation of the People Act.

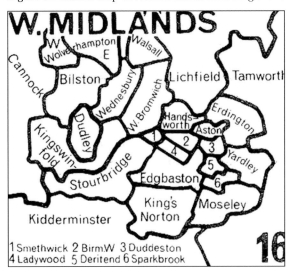

Source: M.Kinnear, *The British Voter, an atlas and survey since 1885*, London, 1968, p 145.
This map is providing the definition of the "West Midlands" for the purposes of this book.
However, no women candidates stood elsewhere for the 1918 General Election in the region
now commonly defined as the West Midlands, consisting of the counties of Shropshire,
Staffordshire, Herefordshire, Worcestershire and Warwickshire.

Figure 2: Stourbridge, Smethwick and Ladywood Parliamentary Constituencies, 1918.

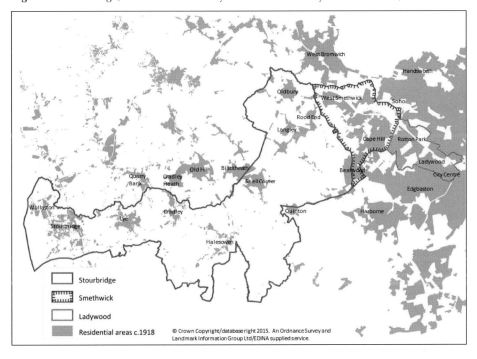

Foreword

HISTORY is littered with women being told what they can and can't do. A hundred years ago there was a whole generation who had been told that they couldn't vote, nor stand for election to Parliament.

It is well known that in the last year of the First World War women finally won the right to vote. What is not so well known is that they were still legally barred from standing as Parliamentary candidates. This was put right on the 21 November 1918 when Royal Assent was given to an Act of Parliament enabling women to stand on the same basis as men. It was one of the shortest Acts of Parliament on record.

Within days the government called a General Election. Seventeen women put their names forward, three of them covering constituencies within walking distance of my childhood home in Smethwick. Having been told what they couldn't do, these women were determined to show the male candidates what they could do. *Taking on the Men* tells the story of those three local candidates, here in the West Midlands.

I feel quite honoured to have campaigned in the very same streets and neighbourhoods as the world-famous Christabel Pankhurst and the formidable Mary Macarthur. In 1918 both these women campaigned to enter Parliament in constituencies which are now partially subsumed into the Warley constituency where I grew up and cut my political teeth as a councillor.

It is a century since Sophia Duleep Singh the granddaughter of Maharaja Ranjit Singh, who ruled the Sikh empire from 1801 to 1839, and the goddaughter of Queen Victoria, campaigned for women to have the right to vote in this country. We should not underestimate the work that has since gone into making Parliament gradually come to look more like the people it serves. We now have 208 female MPs sitting in the House of Commons making up a record high of 32% as well as a rise in the number of Black and minority ethnic and Lesbian, Gay, Bisexual and Trans MPs. I am proud that it is the Labour Party leading the way with 119 female MPs (45% of all Labour MPs) but there is still a long way to go and much to do.

As a girl, I was blessed with a father and mother who stressed that I could achieve great things if I really tried: being female and a Sikh may have made things harder, but they had a real belief that this wonderful country could and would provide opportunities.

I was also blessed to go to an exceptional secondary school for girls just over the border in Birmingham, now in the constituency that I represent in Parliament. At the time Lordswoods Girls School had a charismatic head teacher, Mrs Brown, who believed in "educating the girls of today to be the women of tomorrow". Both parents and school worked together to ensure that I had the self-confidence to put myself forward into the political arena.

The fight to remove obstacles and provide opportunities is not over. I remember my first local Labour Party meetings being dominated by middle-aged men. Many of them had given sterling service, sometimes for decades, to their local communities, however it was always good when a woman spoke up and offered a female perspective.

I continued to experience barriers and in some cases, blatant misogyny, even as a Councillor in the Cabinet, where I was told by men not to concern myself with certain issues or debates and instead go home to look after my kids.

The pioneering women featured in David's book had to overcome enormous obstacles. Whilst the Liberal-Unionist coalition eventually endorsed Christabel Pankhurst as the only woman Coalition candidate, their support was not exactly fulsome. Christabel was able to muster several famous suffragettes, including her mother Emmeline, but she received scant support from the Unionist big guns or from the local party.

Mary Macarthur, the heroine of the Black Country chain-makers dispute, had to face a most odious campaign of slander and sexism from a "false flag" candidate who was secretly financed by Unionist big business. Sadly, these were the last few weeks of Mary's astonishingly happy marriage. Her husband, himself an MP, lost his seat in the same election and died of influenza a few weeks later. Mary contracted cancer and died three years later. Had she lived, she would have almost certainly been in a future Labour cabinet, possibly even Labour Leader.

Margery Corbett Ashby bravely took on the Chamberlain political machine in Ladywood, Birmingham. Her opponent was Neville, later Prime Minister, who treated her with disdain in public. However, in his private letters Neville did express some initial concern and it is noticeable that, at the very least, the Unionist campaign uniquely, in Ladywood, addressed women's issues: Corbett Ashby's intervention made a difference.

Both Macarthur and Corbett Ashby had another issue that needed addressing during the rigours of a campaign. Both were mothers of very young children. They were balancing the demands of the campaign with worries about childcare. Things haven't changed so much and political parties claiming to want more women candidates always need to remember the pressures on mothers and those with other caring responsibilities.

As I look at my young children and think about the opportunities and challenges they face I hope that they use the lessons those before them have learnt as a springboard to demand more and to build on those successes.

David's book is a vital contribution to this learning process. It serves as a reminder that the road to women's representation was a long one, with many real sacrifices along the way. It shows us how far we have come but also how far we still must go. I know that I would never have become Britain's first woman Sikh MP without the commitment of those that went before me.

It is important for women and all of us to know what has happened in the past and where we have come from and in this book David has clearly and eloquently captured this for future generations. Through a vivid presentation of the precious and often precarious steps taken more than a hundred years ago, *Taking on the Men* is necessary reading for all of us who seek to protect the gains and progress made and pursue a genuinely representative House of Commons and gender equality across the country.

Preet Gill MP
House of Commons
November 2018

Chapter One

The Road to 1918

THE economist John Maynard Keynes quoted a Conservative friend who described the House of Commons elected in 1918 as "a lot of hard faced men who look as if they had done very well out of the war."[1] Of the 1,625 candidates for the 707 seats across the four countries of the United Kingdom, just 17 were women, none of whom subsequently sat as MPs.[2] The Coalition won 478 of the 602 seats in Great Britain; favoured candidates had been issued with a "Coupon" signed by both Prime Minister Lloyd George and the Leader of the Conservative Party, Bonar Law. No woman candidate, not even the fiercely pro-Coalition, Christabel Pankhurst, was issued with a Coupon. Only one woman was elected but she joined her 73 Sinn Fein colleagues in meeting separately as the *Dáil Éireann*, Ireland's putative Parliament, so never sat with the "hard faced men".

Three of the unsuccessful women contested neighbouring constituencies for different parties in the West Midlands: Christabel Pankhurst, Women's Party (Coalition), Smethwick; Mary Macarthur, Labour,

---

1   Keynes, J.M., *The Economic Consequences of Peace*, 1919, republished Lanham: Start Classics, 2014. Ebook Library. Web. 20 Aug. 2015 p123.

2   A full list of the first seventeen women candidates with results and biographies can be found in Appendix One.

Stourbridge; and, Margery Corbett Ashby, Liberal, Birmingham, Ladywood.

Each had to contend with older, paternalistic, entrenched male local opposition. Corbett Ashby, aged 36, was faced with the civic paternalism of Neville Chamberlain, aged 49, former Lord Mayor and son of Joseph Chamberlain. Mary Macarthur, aged 38, opposed the sitting MP, industrial Quaker paternalist John Wilson, aged 60, a partner in one of the constituency's major employers. Christabel Pankhurst, aged 38, arrived in Smethwick and promptly deposed the selected Unionist candidate, Major Thompson, aged 67, who was a well-established paternalistic employer and municipal "worthy". She lost against John E. Davison, aged 49, a national organiser for a major trade union with strong local family connections.

The three women candidates in the West Midlands each had differing views of women's suffrage. Christabel Pankhurst is best known for working with her mother Emmeline in the very militant suffragette movement. Mary Macarthur was committed to votes for all men and women, in 1909 being a notable member of the Adult Suffrage League.[3] Margery Corbett Ashby was a suffragist. Writing in 1978 to commemorate the 50th anniversary of the equal enfranchisement of women in 1928, Corbett Ashby pointedly reminded readers that too much attention was focussed on the militancy of the suffragettes, which she believed had set their cause back. It is worth noting that there was a long running and bitter hostility between Macarthur and Pankhurst, which, earlier in the year, Macarthur had placed into the hands of lawyers. There is no evidence to suggest that Pankhurst's decision to contest Smethwick may have been taken with Macarthur's candidacy in the neighbouring constituency in mind, but it remains a possibility.

The 1918 General Election was an extraordinary time when extraordinary things could happen. There were clearly high hopes that

---

3   Bondfield, M., *A Life's Work*, London, 1948, p85.

one of those extraordinary things would be the election of women to Parliament following the extension of the franchise, possibly with a very different agenda to that set by men. It didn't happen in 1918, and for the next 74 years, women never held more than 5%, averaging about 25, of the 600 or so seats in the House of Commons.[4]

The thirtieth Parliament of the United Kingdom was dissolved on 25 November 1918; it had been the longest Parliament since the 1801 Act of Union. This was just a fortnight after the Armistice with Germany. The election was held Saturday 14 December with the votes counted and results declared on Saturday 28 December, in order for absent voters on active service to take part. The election in 1918 was very different from the previous two General Elections, both held in 1910. The Representation of the People Act 1918 had made important changes to the way people could vote and who could vote: it abolished plural voting, mandated that all polls be held on the same day, experimented with proportional representation for university seats, introduced postal and proxy voting for servicemen, lowered the age of voting for servicemen to nineteen, redistributed Parliamentary seats on a more equitable basis, extended the franchise to all men over twenty-one and, with some exceptions, gave women over thirty years old the vote. The new register had been published on 1 October 1918 and there was an expectation that an election would be held before the end of the year.[5/6]

Women had been specifically barred from voting for Parliamentary candidates in the 1832 Great Reform Act, which specified that only 'male persons' could vote, presumably with the assumption that they would not

---

4 Keen, R., for House of Commons Library, *Women in Parliament and Government*, SN01250, London, 23 March 2015.

5 *The Times Guide to the House of Commons 1919*, London, 1919, Reprinted 2004, p8.

6 Women over thirty were not enfranchised on the same basis as men; the 1918 Act restricted the vote to women who were local government electors or the wives of local government electors. It has been estimated that about 22% of women over thirty, mainly working class or unmarried women were excluded. See Harold H. Smith, *The British Women's Suffrage Campaign 1866-1928*, Harlow, 1998, revised second edition, 2010 pp90-91.

be eligible to stand themselves.[7] The women's suffrage clauses in various local government acts of 1869, 1888, and 1894 saw women successfully standing for election to school boards, as poor law guardians, and eventually on parish and district councils.[8]

However, the Representation of the People Act of 1918 had not resolved one major issue: were women able to offer themselves as candidates for Parliament and to take their seats, if elected?

In May 1918 Miss Nina Boyle, a member of the Women's Freedom League, had presented herself as a candidate for the Keighley by-election. The returning officer declared both her submitted nomination papers out of order on technical grounds which had nothing to do with gender. He would have accepted her nomination but the question of her qualification would be "determinable elsewhere".[9] Within weeks the Independent Labour Party added Margaret Bondfield and Ethel Snowden to their list of Parliamentary candidates. In August Mary Macarthur was selected as Labour candidate for Stourbridge.[10] Questions were soon being asked in the House of Commons. The lawyers were consulted and Bonar Law announced that "in the unanimous opinion of the Law Officers of England, Scotland and Ireland, a woman is not entitled to be a candidate for Parliament." This led to a lobbying campaign by the women's organisations who found that press and public were sympathetic. In late October 1918, a motion supporting women's representation was put to a Commons vote and carried by 274 to 25. A bill introduced soon after made a "triumphal progress" and received the Royal Assent on 21 November 1918, just four days before the dissolution.[11]

7   Smith, H.H., ibid, p3.

8   Rover, C., *Women's Suffrage and British Politics*, London, 1967, p29.

9   'Miss Boyle's Nomination Papers Invalid.' *Times* [London, England] 20 Apr. 1918: 3. *The Times Digital Archive*. Web. 24 Aug. 2015.

10   Brookes, ibid, p4.

11   How-Martyn, E., on behalf of Women's Election Committee, *The Need for Women Members of Parliament*, London, undated, but with a handwritten note in the copy held in the Museum of London "c.1922".

Despite the end of hostilities, November and December 1918 was a miserable period for families throughout the country. The servicemen had not been demobilised and were still away from home. Each edition of the local newspapers would carry reports of soldiers who had been killed on active service in the last weeks of the war, or died of wounds. Thousands of women workers had been made redundant within days or even hours of the Armistice. Schools were closed and health services overstretched as an influenza pandemic spread. There were still widespread shortages in the shops. Smethwick, for example, with a population of 65,000, had a fifth of the male adult population away on active service, seven hundred families had been bereaved, two hundred within the previous twelve months, and several hundred men had returned wounded and disabled. There was considerable criticism at the time that this was not the moment for an election, but Lloyd George's position as the leader of a government without the support of the bulk of his party, meant that a snap election suited his calculations for political survival. It was against this background that three women chose to contest adjacent Parliamentary seats in the West Midlands.

Chapter Two

Christabel Pankhurst in Smethwick

O F THE three women candidates in the West Midlands and the fifteen contesting seats in Great Britain, Christabel Pankhurst came closest to winning. She had the support of the Coalition but this fell short of offering her the "Coupon".

Christabel Pankhurst arrived to open her campaign in Smethwick on Wednesday 27 November 1918. She was taking on the local patriarchy found on both sides of industry and politics, especially the Unionist, a local "worthy".[12]

It was her first visit to Smethwick. She left after the result was declared on Saturday 28 December. She never returned. In her biography, published posthumously in 1959, referring to the entitlement of women to stand for Parliament in 1918, she simply says "Some [women] had made an eleventh hour attempt, including myself".[13] Pankhurst was not the Coalition's first choice for Smethwick, neither was Smethwick

---

12 "Worthy" was a noun much in use during the 19th and early 20th century to describe notable people in a particular locality, "**n.worthy** (pl **worthies**) … a person important in a particular local sphere: *local worthies*". From the *Pocket Oxford English Dictionary*, Oxford, 9th edition, 2002, p1073.

13 Pankhurst, C., Ed Lord Pethick-Lawrence, *Unshackled, the story of how we won the vote*, London, 1959, p294.

14

Pankhurst's first choice of constituency. By the time she arrived both Labour and Unionists had well established local candidates in place. However, she was able to dispose of the Unionist candidate, a local "worthy", and probably not well-known, nor with political connections, beyond Smethwick. She received the Coalition's endorsement, but was never actually provided with the "Coupon" letter formally signed by both Lloyd George and Bonar Law which identified other approved Coalition candidates.[14]

Smethwick was a rapidly growing industrial town. It had been created a municipal borough in 1899, a county borough in 1906 and a Parliamentary constituency in its own right for the 1918 General Election.[15] Many commentators made the mistake of thinking that Smethwick was part of Birmingham, but the town had made the decision on successive occasions not to be absorbed by its larger neighbour, or, for that matter, into the Chamberlains' political machine that controlled the city. Until 1918 Parliamentary representation had been shared with the Staffordshire county division of Handsworth, a Unionist stronghold. In the January 1910 election the Liberals put up a candidate for Handsworth but the Unionists swept in with 14,594 votes against 9,488, and were then returned unopposed in the December 1910 election.[16]

When the new Smethwick constituency voters list was published in October 1918 it showed a total of 32,964 voters; 20,182 men and 12,726 women. Over a quarter of the male voters (5,393) were registered as absent voters.[17]

In February 1918, an editorial in the *Smethwick Telephone* pointed out that the Representation of the People Act, which had received Royal

---

14 Craig, F.W.S., *British Parliamentary Election Results 1918-1949*, Glasgow, 1969, entry 230 p241, footnote.

15 Inslip, K.W., *Smethwick from hamlet to County Borough, a brief history*, Smethwick, 1966 pp10, 14.

16 *The Times Guide to the House of Commons 1911*, p86.

17 'The List of Electors', *Smethwick Telephone*, 12 October 1918.

Assent the previous Friday, "marked a new chapter in the political history of Smethwick". The local Labour Party had already selected their candidate, John E. Davison, a trade union official, who had been born in the borough and worked there as an iron-moulder. There was also the expectation that the Unionists would put forward Major Samuel Nock Thompson.[18] These men presented formidable opponents for Pankhurst. In a rapidly growing and changing town both had families who had lived in the area for several generations.

Immediately after the election was announced a pen sketch of the "Coalition candidate", contributed by "a native", was offered in the local paper. Pankhurst was not mentioned as that same weekend she announced her candidacy for Westbury in Wiltshire. The pen portrait started with a quotation from Addison: "Tis not in mortals to command success, But we'll do more, Sempronious; we'll deserve it." The writer then went on to describe knowing of Thompson's contribution to the civic and commercial life of the town over many years. Samuel Nock Thompson was born in 1851, making him 67 by 1918. His father was a maltster and miller in Smethwick who originally wanted his son to go into the law. His early education had been at "F. W. Astle's Academy, a fine old seminary, from which quite a number of Smethwick's worthies sprang." The unexpected death of an uncle meant that Thompson had to change course and join the family business. From there on Thompson devoted his life to the family brewing business which had its headquarters in Rolfe Street, the Blue Gates public house in Smethwick High Street, and maltings in London, Bristol, Taunton, Wiltshire, Shropshire and Peterborough. He was also involved with a metal and bell founders based in the town. His commitment to the civic, sporting, and philanthropic life of the town was phenomenal, as was his involvement in the voluntary battalion of the Worcestershire Regiment, from which he derived his title of "Major". The article ends with a simple prophecy: "There is this

18 'Parliamentary Representation of Smethwick', *Smethwick Telephone*, 16 February 1918.

about the election in this new constituency – and it is in keeping with the endeavour in this article to steer clear of partisanship: it is bound to be represented by a native."[19]

The Labour Candidate, John E. Davison, aged 49, and, according to his biographer "C.J.", in the following week's *Smethwick Telephone*, "in the prime of his life", had links with Smethwick and the iron industries that went back at least two generations. Both his father and grandfather had worked in local foundries. His grandfather joined the Friendly Society of Iron Founders in 1847 and his father in 1868. He joined in 1890 and within two years was holding local office. He went on to become a full-time national officer and was widely respected for the work he did on behalf of its members. During the war Davison was very active in supporting voluntary recruitment, even speaking at recruitment meetings. As a member of the Trades Union Advisory Committee he had been responsible for easing many difficult situations. "C.J." praised Davison's oratorical skills and speculated that "it is still possible that in the Parliament to meet in January next, Smethwick will speak through the lips of a Smethwick man."[20]

What Christabel Pankhurst lacked in local connections she made up through her surname and her connections, mainly via her mother, Emmeline. For many years, the Pankhursts had been leading figures in the suffragette movement. Shortly after war was declared in 1914 Christabel returned from exile in Paris and the whole energies of the Women's Social and Political Union were directed to supporting the war effort. When challenged that the WSPU should continue to press for votes for women, Christabel would impatiently reply, "Cannot discuss that now." The former suffragettes then "travelled the country castigating slackers, sneering at conscientious objectors, demanding

---

19   'Pen Sketch of the Coalition Candidate' *Smethwick Telephone*, 23 November, 1918.
20   'The John E Davison (the Labour Candidate)', *Smethwick Telephone*, 30 November, 1918.

Asquith's resignation and the internment of all enemy aliens, denouncing industrial strikes and talk of a negotiated peace, advocating universal conscription and a 'knockout blow'."[21]

As the war progressed Lloyd George took over from Asquith as Liberal Prime Minister, leading a Coalition government. Lloyd George took a more flexible view of women's suffrage than Asquith and included a clause enabling some women to vote in the new Representation of the People Bill. The Pankhursts began to think of new opportunities for Christabel. During a business breakfast with Lloyd George in 1917 Emmeline impressed on him that she and Christabel intended to "work harder than ever to keep women out of the clutches of R. MacDonald & Co" with a programme that would "carry the best elements of the working class with us."[22] Early in November 1917 the WSPU's weekly newspaper *Britannia* announced that "THE WOMEN'S SOCIAL AND POLITICAL UNION will henceforward be known as THE WOMEN'S PARTY." Inside was "the women's programme for the war and after" which spread over two pages, much of which focussed on Britain's place in the world and the prosecution of the war, with an examination of social issues such as divorce, equality, housing, and education appearing in the second half.[23]

The Women's Party campaign was launched at the Queen's Hall in London on Tuesday 19 November 1918. Emmeline Pankhurst said that "We have decided to fight a constituency, and we have chosen our candidate. The candidate we feel to be best fitted to be our spokeswoman is my eldest daughter, Christabel Pankhurst."[24] The following day *The Times* reported that "Miss Pankhurst's constituency had not yet

---

21   Mitchell, D., *Queen Christabel, A biography of Christabel Pankhurst*, London, 1977, p249-50.

22   Ibid, p268.

23   *Britannia*, 2 November 1917.

24   'To win the peace', *Britannia*, 22 November 1918.

been chosen but would be announced shortly."[25] Her speech was carried in the following Friday's edition of the Women's Party weekly newspaper *Britannia* together with a photograph of Christabel describing her as the "Women's Party Candidate for the Westbury Division of Wiltshire."[26]

Even as the *Britannia* presses were rolling on the Thursday there were contrary developments: Lloyd George wrote to Bonar Law asking him to see Christabel Pankhurst with a view to her fighting Westbury. "Northcliffe is especially keen and promises to run a special edition of the *Evening News* in that area to promote Miss Pankhurst's candidature ... I am not sure we have any women candidates and think it highly desirable that we should ... The Women's Party, of which Miss Pankhurst is the leader, has been extraordinarily useful, as you know, to the Government – especially in the industrial areas where there has been trouble in the last two very trying years. They have fought the Bolshevist and Pacifist element with great skill, tenacity, and courage, and I know especially in Glasgow and S. Wales their intervention produced remarkable results."

On the same day Christabel Pankhurst wrote to Lloyd George saying she had changed her mind and that "something very much better than Westbury is now available, but for a little difficulty you can clear up." The "something better" was Smethwick, the "little difficulty" was Thompson. The following Saturday Bonar Law wrote to Christabel Pankhurst expressing appreciation for her support during the war and "For that reason I should personally be glad to see you returned to the House, and hope you will be able to find a suitable constituency."[27] Whether Bonar Law knew at that stage Pankhurst was intending to switch her candidacy to Smethwick is unclear. What is clear is that neither the voters of Westbury, nor of Smethwick, nor Thompson himself, were aware of what was unfolding in London.

25 'A Tragic Farce'. *Times* [London, England] 20 Nov. 1918: 10. *The Times Digital Archive.* Web. 31 July 2015.
26 'Miss Christabel Pankhurst' *Britannia*, 22 November 1918.
27 Mitchell, ibid, p272.

The following Monday, the Women's Party arrived in Smethwick accompanied by reporters from, among other newspapers, Northcliffe's *Daily Mail,* who reported that Pankhurst applied herself in a "business-like manner to the preliminary work, engaging committee rooms, interviewing workers and arranging meetings."[28] The following Friday the local paper was apparently quite bemused by the opening of the campaign: "A lady holding a large Chinese lantern mounted a table outside of the Blue Gates Hotel, and began to speak to a blind news-vendor, a policeman and a reporter for her audience. Thus began the campaign on behalf of Miss Christabel Pankhurst, on Monday night. The audience was a hundred before the introductory words were finished, and then for an hour the first phase of the educational work which the Women's Party have undertaken was continuing at white heat. It was a unique – if not historic – gathering."[29]

Pankhurst herself did not speak at that meeting, the principal speaker being Phyllis Ayrton. Elsewhere in the same edition, it was reported "Miss Christabel Pankhurst paid her first visit to Smethwick on Wednesday. She had never been in the constituency before, and this debut was for the benefit of the press photographers, who were able to 'improve the shining hour'. The candidate and Mrs Drummond formed the centre of the pictures, while Miss Pankhurst was a charming 'subject' as she stood on the step of her motor. She was able to furnish a splendid story to the interviewers."

A photograph of Pankhurst was supplied to the *Telephone,* the same severe one of Pankhurst that had appeared in *Britannia* complete with mortar board and academic gown the Friday before announcing

---

28 'Miss Pankhurst. Birmingham Campaign Today', *Daily Mail,* London, 26 November 1918.

29 'An Election Surprise Packet, Miss Christabel Pankhurst comes to Smethwick', *Smethwick Telephone,* 30 November 1918.

her candidature for Westbury.[30] This photograph, very much in the suffragette tradition of emphasising the intellectual ability of women, was used to illustrate her election address.

Early on in the campaign it was clear that both Davison and Thompson were equally considered opponents who could not compete with Pankhurst's celebrity. In her speech outside the Blue Gates on the Monday evening, Phyllis Ayrton had asked "Would Smethwick not like to be represented by a woman who is known all over the world rather than those who have but a local reputation?" The *Daily Mail* reported that Smethwick had been shrouded in mist in which "The Coalitionist and the Labour man are both invisible".[31] The Women's Party justified their decision to contest Smethwick on the basis that it was a new constituency and "therefore there can be no suggestion that any party or person has a better claim than Miss Christabel Pankhurst to represent the voters of Smethwick."[32] They told a Birmingham newspaper that they had gone through all 700 constituencies, studied the conditions and candidates, and came to the conclusion that Smethwick was the constituency for them.[33]

Initially the assumption was that there would be a three way fight for the Smethwick seat. Thompson himself made it clear that he expected to remain a candidate.[34] Behind the scenes it seems that there was frantic activity with a view to getting Thompson to stand down. When he did stand down, and in doing so nominating Pankhurst, it was

---

30 'Miss Christabel Pankhurst's Candidature', *Smethwick Telephone*, 30 November, 1918. Having been a press officer for over 50 years, the author can see very clearly that the local newspaper staff were not happy with their treatment by the Pankhurst team.

31 'Miss Pankhurst, Mother's Appeal to Women', *Daily Mail*, London, 27 November 1918.

32 'A new constituency', *Britannia*, 29 November 1918.

33 'From the Birmingham Daily Mail, Mrs Pankhurst at Smethwick' reprinted in *Britannia*, 22 November 1918.

34 'The Election.' *Times* [London, England] 28 Nov. 1918: 7+. *The Times Digital Archive*. Web. 31 July 2015.

presented as a patriotic[35], magnanimous[36], and generous[37], gesture. It was widely understood at the time that Pankhurst and Thompson had met privately to discuss his continuing candidature and that Thompson's decision had followed the receipt of a letter from Bonar Law asking him to stand down[38] but it was not until many years later that a fuller account became available. Sebastian Hosgood, a Birmingham solicitor, or his wife Phyllis, wrote a still unpublished, and now possibly lost, biography which revealed his involvement in the episode. Initially, the Pankhursts had asked him to be the election agent, which he refused. However, he did arrange a meeting between Pankhurst and Thompson. Just when this meeting took place is not known, but certainly after Pankhurst had announced her candidacy. At the meeting Pankhurst got straight to the point and asked Thompson to stand down. He said this was impossible on the basis that he had been nursing the constituency for some time and suggested she should do so. Hosgood recorded "It was arranged that the Major should consult his committee … A very frank discussion took place and it was decided that the Leaders should be asked to decide … I realised that the matter was of national importance in that the women's vote throughout the country meant much to the party and I agreed to go to London." Hosgood went to London and met with Bonar Law who left a meeting of "French generals and statesmen" to see him. Lloyd George did not join them but Bonar Law drafted a letter to Thompson "with the necessary guidance" which he then discussed with Lloyd George. "I was told of the contents, a recommendation

---

35 'Major S.N. Thompson Withdraws. Decision to Stand Aside for Miss Pankhurst', *Birmingham Daily Post*, 4 December 1918. Thompson was honoured for this move by being made a Freeman of the Borough 9th July 1920.

36 'Major Thompson nominates Miss Pankhurst', *Britannia*, 6 December, 1918.

37 'The Major', *Smethwick Telephone*, 7 December, 1918.

38 'Coalition Support Of Miss Pankhurst.' *Times* [London, England] 4 Dec. 1918: 12. *The Times Digital Archive*. Web. 31 July 2015.

that Major Thompson should retire."[39] The *Daily Mail* speculated that Thompson may step down in a report datelined Monday 2 December.[40] It is not clear whether Hosgood returned from London with the letter but its arrival on Tuesday 3 December led to Thompson's immediate withdrawal. Whilst Thompson himself went to considerable lengths to appear to support Pankhurst by signing her nomination paper and chairing campaign meetings, the *Smethwick Telephone* reported that the news was "received on Tuesday afternoon with great surprise, not to say indignation." There were animated discussions at the Unionist committee rooms and the decision to abandon their campaign was taken with considerable reluctance.[41] Whether the Unionist machinery swung behind Pankhurst is not clear. Her biographer reports that "she had not endeared herself to the local Conservatives", she had flu and was missing key workers, suggesting that she entered the last ten days or so of the campaign depressed.[42]

Pankhurst attracted considerable national press interest. Northcliffe gave her extensive coverage in the *Daily Mail* with articles appearing on at least nine occasions over the two-week campaign with the later ones being by-lined "from our woman reporter". Other national newspapers ran supportive articles including *The Times*, *The Globe*, and the *Daily*

---

39 Mitchell, ibid, p273. Mitchell refers to a "P.G. Hosgood" rather than Sebastian, however there is no "P.G. Hosgood" listed as a solicitor in Birmingham. However Sebastian Hosgood is listed in the 1916 edition of *Kelly's Directory for Birmingham* p1037 who was a partner in Docker, Hosgood and Co at 10 Newhall Street, Birmingham. He was married to a Phyllis Gertrude and it may be that for some reason Mitchell got the name and initials mixed up. (Email from G. Hartley 20 April 2018) No Hosgood has been recorded as a member of the Birmingham City Council or the Smethwick Borough Council, nor is there any other record available suggesting political activity. Sebastian Hosgood represented a number of large Birmingham companies in various litigation throughout the 1910s and 1920s and it may well be that the connection had been through the Chamberlains.

40 'Woman v Woman, Miss Pankhurst's Labour Opponent' *Daily Mail*, London, 3 December 1918.

41 'Notes in Brief', *Smethwick Telephone*, 7 December, 1918.

42 Mitchell, ibid, p275.

Express.[43] The Women's Party weekly newspaper was pressed into service as a campaigning tool with exhortations to vote for Pankhurst on the front, and reprints of sympathetic articles from other newspapers.[44] Pankhurst's main campaign was against the threat of Bolshevism and demanded a punitive peace with Germany. The keynote of her home policy was industrial harmony, and 'Britain for the British'.[45] Her slogans were "Union Jack v Red Flag",[46] and "make Germany pay".[47] In this she was not alone; it was the theme of every Coalition candidate throughout Great Britain. However, from the evidence available from the local newspapers of the time, *Britannia*, and other reports of the campaign, there was very little effort to raise specifically women's issues. Pankhurst said that electricity would make women's lives easier, but with no indication of how Pankhurst's election would help achieve this.[48] Pankhurst explained this omission by saying " … whatever might be the case in other constituencies; the women electors of Smethwick were showing no apathy now. Although they realised the importance of social questions, especially housing, they were primarily concerned with the German question."[49] Pankhurst upset local discharged soldiers by claiming that they were supporting her, "we strongly resent this misrepresentation of the true facts."[50]

---

43 'The First Woman MP? Victory Song for Miss Pankhurst', *Daily Express*, London, 6 December 1918.

44 Other writers, including Mitchell, have relied on these reprints as a source material. The coverage in the local newspapers was much more balanced.

45 'Miss Pankhurst, Birmingham Campaign Today', *Daily Mail*, London, 26 November 1918.

46 'Union Jack v. Red Flag, Miss Pankhurst's Battle Cry', *Daily Mail*, London, 9 December 1918.

47 'Make Germany Pay, Miss Pankhurst's solution', *Daily Mail*, London 11 December 1918.

48 'Electric Homes, Miss Pankhurst's Vision of the Future', *Daily Mail*, London, 13 December 1918.

49 'Make Germany Pay, Miss Pankhurst's Solution', *Daily Mail*, London, 11 December 1918.

50 'Miss Pankhurst's Claim, discharged soldiers resent a misrepresentation', *Evening Despatch*, Birmingham, 6 December 1918.

Davison took care in his reaction to Pankhurst. He resented being described as a Bolshevik. "He had been told he was a Bolshevist. He wanted to say that he was one of their own folk – born in the Spon Lane district, reared amongst them, partly schooled with them, and would probably have continued his association throughout his life in the district had it not been for the fact that through economic circumstances his family were compelled to seek their living elsewhere, in Sheffield. 'I am no Bolshevist. I am a sane, practical, trade union leader – one who believes in law and order, and constitutional government'".[51] He pointed out that Labour had worked for constitutional reform, but, in contrast to Pankhurst, "without breaking a single window, firing a single pillar box, or burning down a single church."[52] Reacting to the news that Thompson had withdrawn, Davison said "This is the most diabolical political conspiracy that has ever been perpetrated on the electors of any division." Referring to the doubt about the funding of the Women's Party he displayed a cheque from his union, saying "'There is no dubiety, no equivocation about the source from which my election expenses come. They come from the hard-earned pence of the men in whose midst I have lived and worked during the whole course of my existence.' He left the other candidates to tell the audience the source from which their campaign expenses came."[53] Davison's other weapon was his fellow Labour candidate from the neighbouring Stourbridge constituency, Mary Macarthur, who spoke at a meeting on his behalf at the Smethwick Empire.[54]

The national press and some Birmingham papers believed that Pankhurst was going to win. The *Daily Mail* gave glowing reports from

---

51 'Mr. Davison's Candidature', *Smethwick Telephone*, 14 December 1918.

52 'Miss C. Pankhurst's Campaign.' *Times* [London, England] 14 Dec. 1918: 10. *The Times Digital Archive*. Web. 31 July 2015.

53 'Mr. Davison on Major Thompson's Withdrawal', *Smethwick Telephone*, 7 December 1918.

54 Advertisement 'General Election 1918, The Labour Campaign', Smethwick Telephone, 7 December 1918.

meetings and even on one occasion claimed that schoolchildren had composed a song with the words "Vote, vote, vote for Christabel, Christie's sure to win the day. When the soldiers come home with a double-barrelled gun, they'll blow old Davison away."[55] This creativity was not referred to in the local press. The *Birmingham Daily Post* predicted "there is little doubt that she [Pankhurst] will be, if not the first, at any rate among the first, women to sit in the House of Commons."[56] Other local papers were not so certain and these articles were, unsurprisingly, not reprinted in *Britannia*. The Birmingham *Evening Despatch* accused her of a "raging, tearing" campaign. It acknowledged that she was drawing "crowded houses" but cautioned "whether all the people she amuses nightly will vote for her remains to be seen." The paper was critical of her anti-Bolshevism which dominated her campaign. She saw "pro-Germans on every street corner" and refused to answer an awkward question when she was told the questioner was "pro-German". The paper asserted that there was "nothing constructive in the programme of Miss Pankhurst, but of self-confidence there is an astonishing surplus … 'When I am member for Smethwick' is a sentence she repeats with nauseating repetition."[57]

On polling day *The Times* reported "Local opinion regards the result of tomorrow's poll as a foregone conclusion. It is believed her majority will be large. She can rely on a fair share of support from absent voters." *The Times* argued that some Labour supporters had expressed their support for her. This claim rested on the sole case of a Labour councillor who had written to Pankhurst saying he, his wife and soldier son would support her.[58] Neither the *Smethwick Telephone* nor the Smethwick edition

---

55 'Miss Pankhurst, Success Against Apathy', *Daily Mail*, London, 7 December, 1918.

56 'The Campaign in the Midlands', *Birmingham Daily Post* 10 December 1918 reprinted in *Britannia* 13 December 1918.

57 'Election Notes and Points, Miss Christabel Pankhurst's "Raging, Tearing" Campaign at Smethwick', *Evening Despatch*, Birmingham, 10 December 1918.

58 "Miss C. Pankhurst's Campaign." *Times* [London, England] 14 Dec. 1918: 10. *The Times Digital Archive*. Web. 31 July 2015.

of *The Weekly News* offered predictions of the result. In their edition published on polling day the *Smethwick Telephone* gave extraordinarily good coverage to Pankhurst and made no mention of Mary Macarthur's intervention on Davison's behalf the previous Sunday.

When the votes were counted on Saturday 28 December Davison won with a majority of 775 representing a margin of 4.4%.

Candidate	Party	Votes	%
Davison	Labour	9389	52.2
Pankhurst	Coalition	8614	47.8
Majority		775	4.4

Total electorate: 32,964; women voters 12,726

With 8,614 votes Pankhurst scored the highest vote of any woman candidate. Davison expressed his delight at beating the Coalition saying "I am more proud of the fact that Labour in Smethwick has risen to a sense of its responsibilities and defeated the Coalition than I am of having beaten the woman candidate." The result was "an emphatic and effective protest against the arrogant presumption of any person, be they ever so eminent, who dared to come down to a constituency and tell people what political opinions they were to hold. It was a protest against the foisting upon a constituency of a candidate not of the people's own choice."[59] The local Unionists made their views known to the *Smethwick Telephone* who reported "that if the Major had persisted in his candidature he would have been the chosen representative."[60] Pankhurst blamed her late arrival in the campaign, the short time that she had after officially being declared the Coalition candidate, and took comfort from what had been achieved in a fortnight. She predicted that it would not be long before she would be in the House of Commons.[61]

---

59 'Mr John E. Davison, M.P., and His Supporters', *Smethwick Telephone*, 4 January 1919.
60 'The Candidates and the Result', *Smethwick Telephone*, 4 January 1919.
61 'Miss Pankhurst's View of the Result', *Smethwick Telephone*, 4 January 1919.

Writing in 2014, Nicoletta Gullace of the University of New Hampshire, has attempted to explain Pankhurst's defeat. Drawing heavily on the biased collection of press cuttings from *Britannia* she concludes that had the franchise been widened to include women over twenty-one rather than over thirty, she would have won. This is speculation, with Gullace accepting, and sometimes enhancing, the carefully curated myths that Pankhurst created at the time.[62]

Subsequent elections demonstrated that post-war Smethwick was a marginal constituency. In 1922 Davison retained the seat with a majority of 382, a margin of 1.4%. In 1923 the margin was 9.4%, in 1924 it fell back to 4.6%.[63]

Pankhurst was right in saying that she did not have time to mount an effective challenge, but that was exaggerated by her last-minute dithering over Westbury. She had known the new electoral geography since February. She had no base in Smethwick, there was not a local

---

62 Nicoletta E. Gullace, "Christabel Pankhurst and the Smethwick Election: right wing feminism, the Great War and the ideology of consumption", *Women's History Review*, 23:3, p330-346, London, 2014. This paper contains numerous inaccuracies which Gullace has accepted in good faith from Pankhurst's material, but sometimes adapting to make her case. For example, on page 339 she says "Testimonies told of families with their soldier sons, issuing forth together to vote for Christabel … ." This is based on the singular recorded case of one father, a councillor, saying that he, his wife and his soldier son, again singular, would be supporting Pankhurst. On page 340 Gullace asserts that, "Christabel was wildly popular among a set of patriotic, independent munitions girls". During the election period these munition "girls" were in the process of facing an abrupt redundancy by hard faced employers who had exploited them whilst their husbands and brothers had been conscripted. Apart from supportive articles written for the Northcliffe press, which were little more than propaganda, there is no evidence to show that this was the case, certainly not from the local reporters on the ground. No academic study of Pankhurst in Smethwick should rely on *Britannia* as anything other than a highly selective publicity vehicle.

63 Smethwick subsequently had a mixed political history. In 1926 Oswald Mosley won a by-election for Labour and continued as the MP for the area until 1931 when he set up The New Party, the forerunner of the British Union of Fascists. In 1945 it had the dubious distinction of having the shortest serving MP ever, and the first by-election of the 1945 Parliament, following the death in a car accident of Alfred Dobbs less than twenty-four hours after being elected. In 1964 it rose to national, even international prominence, when Peter Griffiths, Conservative candidate, was elected on what his opponents believed was an overtly racist campaign. He lost the next election in 1966 to Andrew Faulds. The constituency was abolished in 1974 when it became part of Warley East with Faulds continuing as MP.

branch of her party, nor its forerunner the WSPU. Her campaign team were, like her, visitors and inexperienced. She upset the local Unionists by getting the local "worthy" ditched. She outraged discharged soldiers by assuming their support. She did not appreciate the scale of the Labour surge that went through towns with a similar industrial base such as West Bromwich and Wednesbury. She was not given the Coupon, had no support from Coalition speakers, nor was she invited to intervene on behalf of the Coalition outside of Smethwick. Deposing one patriarch, she underestimated the other.

Chapter Three

Mary Macarthur in Stourbridge

MACARTHUR'S biographer, Mary Hamilton, declared "Stourbridge is a peculiar constituency. The sleepy market town is the centre of a typical stretch of Black Country territory – an agricultural area, freely dotted with patches of a dreary industrialism: groups of brick-makers, chain makers, hollowware workers and other outlying Birmingham trades."[64] Macarthur addressed, two, three, sometimes four meetings a night travelling over "dark, frost-bound or water logged roads".[65] Hamilton's views about the "peculiarity" of the newly created Stourbridge were shared by many of the people who lived there. The previous Northern Division of Worcestershire was centred on the towns of Halesowen and Oldbury.[66] In July 1917, the Boundary Commission proposed a new county constituency which would also include the Borough of Stourbridge and the Urban District of Lye and

---

64 Hamilton, M.A., *Mary Macarthur A biographical sketch*, London, 1925 p173.
65 Ibid, p174.
66 *Kelly's Directory for Warwickshire and Worcestershire, 1916*, London, 1916 p5 of the Worcester Section. These boundaries were set under the "Redistribution of Seats Act, 1885". Note that Dudley Borough was separately represented as a Parliamentary Borough.

Wollescote.[67] There was an immediate objection to the inclusion of Stourbridge because there were strongly perceived differences between Stourbridge, which was seen as "residential" and which did not share the industries and potential for growth predicted for the rest of the constituency.[68] Appeals to a Commissioner were rejected.[69] It was one of the larger constituencies with 42,205 voters, 16,699 of whom were women.[70]

The new constituency did not include the Black Country areas in which Macarthur had made her name. Hamilton remarks that at each meeting there "would rise a gaunt elderly woman, who lifted her hands and 'testified' to what Mary had done for the sweated woman worker." Cradley Heath and neighbouring areas, where Macarthur had risen to prominence in the 1910 chain makers' dispute, were in the newly formed Kingswinford division of Staffordshire[71] which Labour was to win convincingly.[72] Employment in Oldbury and Halesowen was subtly different from that in the parts of the Black Country that had been at the centre of the 1910 dispute. Whilst there were still many small workshops, though no record of chain making, newer mines with emerging industries such as glass, chemicals, railway rolling stock, and steel extrusion provided large scale employment in Oldbury.[73] Workers in Halesowen were able to travel on a "workman's special" early morning train to the Austin Morris motor factory at Northfield, another large

---

67 *Kelly's Directory for Warwickshire and Worcestershire, 1916*, London, 1916, p4 of the Worcestershire Section.

68 'Oldbury Versus Stourbridge, The New Parliamentary Division', *The Weekly News* 6 July 1917.

69 'The Parliamentary Redistribution Bill, Proceedings at Worcester Enquiry', *The Weekly News* 20 July 1917.

70 'Stourbridge Division', *The Weekly News*, 3 January, 1919.

71 Hamilton, Ibid 173-4.

72 *The Times Guide to the House of Commons 1919*, ibid, p61.

73 Kelly, ibid p206.

scale employer.[74] Stourbridge was a market town, had many small scale employers, but glass, rather than metals, had dominated what industry there was in the town, which set it apart from the rest of the Black Country.[75]

The incumbent MP for the former North Worcestershire constituency, the 62 year-old Right Honourable John William Wilson, provided Macarthur with a formidable opponent. His father was one of two Birmingham Quakers who, in 1851, set up the Albright and Wilson chemical works at Oldbury.

Quaker employers took a great interest in the welfare of their workers. The employees of Albright and Wilson presented an illuminated address to the directors in 1901, the firm's 50th anniversary, to "offer our sincere thanks for your continued interest in our welfare", listing the 80 shilling monthly pension paid to former employees, the £100 life assurance payment that replaced the funeral fund, the bonus scheme which "has enabled us to provide extra comforts to our families", the provision of recreational facilities, the directors' interest in the district and the good relations within the company.[76]

Wilson himself had endowed Bury Hill Park, provided nursing care for the sick poor, had given the employees a convalescent home in the Malvern Hills, and had always attended an annual meeting where he addressed the employees as "fellow phosphorus workers". Each January he greeted the company's pensioners when they returned for a reunion. However, "he would never talk politics in the works and he forbade the exhibition there of election posters." Wilson was first elected to Parliament in 1895 when he was returned as a representative of Joseph

---

74 Christiansen, R., *A Regional History of the Railways of Great Britain, Volume 7, The West Midlands*, first published, 1973, 3rd revised edition Nairn 1991, p112-118 and map inside back cover.

75 Kelly ibid p250.

76 Threlfall, R., *The story of 100 years of phosphorus making 1851-1951*, Oldbury, 1951, p115.

Chamberlain's Liberal Unionist Party, having taken the seat off the Liberal Party.[77]

The Liberal Unionists had emerged during the bitter internal feud which engulfed the Liberal Party over home rule for Ireland after 1887.[78] Chamberlain's Liberal Unionists wanted to gain support from newly enfranchised working class voters with promises of old age pensions, improving homes, compensation for injury at work, a judicial system to handle industrial disputes and a pledge to "deal with alien immigration".[79] By the early 1900s Chamberlain's plan to amalgamate with the Unionists, his promotion of protective import tariffs, "tariff reform" or "colonial preference", led to many Liberal Unionists returning to the Liberal Party, including Wilson.[80] Joseph Chamberlain expressed "indescribable anger" when Wilson, whom he saw as a protégé, standing as a Liberal candidate in North Worcester during the 1906 Liberal landslide.[81]

Wilson was clearly a dominant figure in Oldbury which, with a population of about 30,000, was the largest urban area in the new constituency. The male workforce at the Albright and Wilson works numbered 550 which swelled to 900 as women were taken on during the war.[82] Whilst Mary Macarthur was defending the interests of women munition workers laid off immediately following the Armistice[83], Wilson was hosting a tea party and concert to say farewell to 400 women workers at Albright and Wilson in Oldbury. He pointed out that the war had opened new vocational possibilities for women and joked that they could

---

77   *The Times Guide to the House of Commons 1911*, London 1910, reprinted 2004 p92.

78   Cawood, I., *The Liberal Unionist Party*, London 2012 p1-2.

79   Ibid p206.

80   Ibid p231, 268.

81   Russell, A.K., *The Liberal Landslide, The General Election of 1906* Newton Abbot, 1973, p113.

82   Threlfall, ibid, 179.

83   Hamilton, ibid, pp170-171.

even become Members of Parliament, "amid much laughter".[84] The workforce and their families, together with pensioners, suppliers, and contacts garnered from his community work, obviously gave Wilson an impressive base. Despite considerable, and sometimes bitter Unionist opposition,[85] Wilson had retained his seat in 1906 when standing as a Liberal with a majority of 479, and the two 1910 elections with majorities of 319 and 269, respectively. These were straight fights with the Unionists and demonstrated that he already had a core vote of between seven to eight thousand on the then limited franchise.[86]

During the first three years of the war there was a political truce. The edition of the *County Express* of Stourbridge for Saturday 17 November 1917 saw the wartime restraint shattered: The newly formed "British Workers' League" announced that they had adopted Victor Fisher to be their prospective Parliamentary candidate. In the same edition, there was a second article reporting on a meeting the previous Sunday of trade unionists from the new division, who were planning to contest the seat with a Labour Party candidate. Both reports gave a flavour of what was to come: Fisher believed that lessons had to be learnt by capitalists and workers alike. He foresaw a country in which both would work together to ensure the comforts of life for all. He warned of the "apostles of sedition" saying "there were those amongst them at home who were preaching day in and day out a premature and shameful peace. Like a skilled pianist they played each and every chord of human sensibility." The trade unionists were told the new seat could be won. A speaker said "it was not in the interest of the Labour Party to be deterred from its course by a freak candidate." He reported that the trades union were

---

84 'Women Workers at Messrs Albright and Wilson – Farewell Gathering and Presentations', *Weekly News*, 6 December, 1918.

85 The Unionist *Birmingham Mail* for example carried several cartoons attacking Wilson for establishing a subsidiary in the US to avoid American tariff barriers. See Threlfall, p157 and 161.

86 *The Times Guide to the House of Commons 1911*, ibid, p92.

solidly behind the idea of a Labour candidate "although there might be the defection of a few individual members, those freak platforms were welcome to the type of Labour leader who fraternised with the time worn enemies of Labour and were ready to spend their money to divide the Labour force."[87] Over the next few weeks, there were increasingly angry and abusive letters in the *County Express* and *Weekly News* from both sides.

Fisher clearly had ample financial resources. Throughout the spring of 1918 the *County Express* carried a series of large front page display advertisements announcing the formation of branches and offices in Lye, Oldbury and Halesowen. The BWL propaganda was focussed on Labour. The Independent Labour Party was a "rag tag and bobtail of British Bolsheviks" and personal attacks were made on Ramsey MacDonald the Labour leader and Philip Snowden.[88] Notices of meetings were affixed with slogans saying "No pacifism or pro-Germanism". They also adopted the name "National Democratic and Labour Party", possibly creating more confusion about their antecedents.[89]

Fisher's lavish expenditure was noted, with Mr R Drinkwater, the secretary of the Stourbridge and Lye Trades Council asking "who does finance Mr Fisher?"[90] Evidence has since emerged that may have surprised even Mr Drinkwater. Fisher was largely funded by a number of rich people around Viscount Milner, the controversial Liberal Unionist and associate of Joseph Chamberlain. Milner was a man with complex political views, who himself paid Fisher a salary and expenses from

---

87 'British Workers' League, Candidate for Stourbridge Division, Mr. Victor Fisher Adopted' and 'Stourbridge Parliamentary Division, Labour Party in Favour of Contesting Seat', *County Express,* 17 November 1917.

88 'British Workers' League, Public Meeting at Stourbridge, Speeches by Mr. Victor Fisher and Mr. Havelock Wilson', *County Express,* 20 April 1918.

89 Advertisement 'British Workers' League, The National Democratic and Labour Party', *County Express,* 15 June 1918.

90 'Labour and the Stourbridge Division, Mr. Victor Fisher's Candidature', *The Weekly News,* 23 November 1917.

January 1916 worth about £5,000, or nearly £450,000 in 2018 terms.[91] In 1915 Fisher had worked with Milner and Birmingham Unionist MP Arthur Steel-Maitland to provide Unionist funds for an anti-Labour working class candidate in a Welsh by-election. The evidence may be scanty: one letter that has survived explicitly asks the recipient to destroy it, the sender recognising the sensitivity of such funding.[92] Many NDLP candidates were given a free run, without Unionist opposition, some receiving the "Coupon", including Fisher.[93] Fisher had been preparing the ground with West Midlands Unionism for several months. In October 1918, he had written to Austen Chamberlain repeating a conversation he had had with Neville Chamberlain the day before. He wanted to assure the Chamberlains that he had "practically got the support of the whole of the Trade Unionist movement there", and was asking for his authorisation before approaching the local Unionists not to field a candidate.[94] Given the history between the Chamberlains and Wilson this may have been an opportunity for scores to be settled. But Fisher's considerable resources were to be used mainly against Macarthur.

Mary Macarthur was Labour's second choice. In February 1918, a conference of trade unionists selected 54 year-old Simeon Webb as the prospective Labour candidate for Stourbridge[95] but he had to withdraw in May. A recalled meeting received the nomination from the National Federation of Women Workers of Mary Macarthur, their

---

91 Douglas, R., 'The National Democratic Party and the British Workers' League', *The Historical Journal*, xv 3 (1972), p535.

92 Doyle, B.M., 'Who Paid the Price of Patriotism? The Funding of Charles Stanton during the Merthyr Borough By-Election of 1915', *The English Historical Review*, Vol 109, No 434 (Nov 1994) pp1215-1222. Note the letter from R. MacLeod, penultimate paragraph pp1221-1222.

93 Douglas, ibid, p541.

94 Papers of Austen Chamberlain, Cadbury Research Centre, University of Birmingham, AC12/85. A letter in this collection shows just how deeply embedded Fisher wanted to be within the Birmingham Unionist plans for the next General Election.

95 'Mr. Simeon Webb, Labour's Choice for Stourbridge Division', *County Express*, 9 February 1918.

General Secretary, who was present. Macarthur was a major figure within the emerging Labour movement and had played an important part in building women's trades unionism and subsequently working with the government to improve conditions of women munition workers. She had won a good reputation in the Black Country with her resolute leadership of the chain makers' strike.

Mary Macarthur told the meeting she was not a supporter of the "sex war" but endorsed the whole of the policy laid down by the Labour Party. She was no feminist, but an out and out trade unionist. The meeting adopted her with a "substantial majority". It was not lost on all involved that Macarthur's selection was an historic event. The local newspaper ran the headline "First Woman Candidate?" It commented that "her name is particularly well known to all our readers, as she has never lost touch with the locality." They added "Though she retains her familiar maiden name in her public work, Miss Macarthur is the wife of Mr W.C. Anderson MP, the Labour member for the Attercliffe Division of Sheffield, and they have one child – a little girl nearly three years old."

Later in the week she spoke to women hollowware workers in Lye. She was honoured to have been selected by the "working men of the division, in spite of all the ridicule which might be poured upon them, for no woman had ever sat in Parliament and no woman had ever been nominated by a political party." She was quite against the "anti-man woman" and believed in men and women fighting together. She then speculated about what would happen when she arrived at Westminster, suggesting that the officials might lock the door on her. That wouldn't matter a bit, she would be a pioneer and the mere fact she had been elected would prevent them from locking the doors on any other woman. She was not going to stand merely as a woman, or because she was a woman. If she had to be a candidate for any particular section, she would be the children's candidate and see that they all had a decent chance. She wanted them "to have a better texture of life, a greater share of the sun, more joy and colour in their lives with education as the golden gate that was going to open a new world to our children."[96]

Relations between Macarthur and Christabel Pankhurst, who eventually contested the neighbouring Smethwick seat, were poor. In August 1918, *The Times* reported that a resolution was to be placed before the National Federation of Women Workers' impending conference which was to "protest against the objects and propaganda of the Women's Party, the whole purpose of which tends to create sex antagonism, and resolves to take immediate steps to counteract the Women's Party."[97] The following day the Women's Party responded claiming that one of their principal aims was to resist pacifism and Bolshevism. "Unfortunately, one of the biggest obstacles encountered in this propaganda is the deplorable action of the National Federation of Women Workers, led by Miss Mary Macarthur, who is the wife of Mr W.C. Anderson – the pacifist-Bolshevik MP. Miss Macarthur's organisation … has made common cause with the pacifist-Bolsheviks, and incites women munition workers to act in association with the men strike-mongers and to down tools in company with them."[98] A fortnight later *The Times* published a letter from Macarthur's solicitors objecting to the claim that the Federation had incited women workers to cease work, that there was no justification whatever for the statement and all the efforts of the client and Federation had been directed to prevent stoppages of war work in war-time. The letter continued "They do not believe that this can be done if strife is stirred up between the sexes, as this only accentuates friction in the factory", ending that given the valuable support *The Times* had given their client on many occasions "she therefore doubly regrets

---

96 'Stourbridge Division, Labour Party Conference, Miss Macarthur to Fight the Seat', and 'Miss Mary Macarthur, First Woman Candidate', *County Express*, 18 May 1918.

97 'Women Workers' Demands.' *Times* [London, England] 29 Aug. 1918: 3. *The Times Digital Archive*. Web. 21 July 2015.

98 'Women Workers' Demands'. *Times* [London, England] 30 Aug. 1918: 8. The Times Digital Archive. Web. 21 July 2015.

that the hospitality of your columns should have been abused by a cruel and unjustifiable personal attack upon her."[99] Doubtless similar letters were sent direct to the Women's Party and may have some bearing on Christabel Pankhurst's decision to contest the neighbouring seat in the General Election later that year. Had Fisher not already been in the frame as Coalition candidate, would Pankhurst have challenged Macarthur? The exchange certainly gave an indication of the hostility that existed between the newly enfranchised women leaders. It also demonstrated the similarity in styles of attack between the Women's Party and Fisher's NDLP.

When nominations opened, there were still two unexpected developments in store. The first was for Wilson to be denied the Coalition's "Coupon", despite being an incumbent Liberal; the Coupon went to Fisher. This came as a surprise to Wilson and his supporters but throughout the remainder of the campaign he made it clear he would support the Coalition "in getting through reforms for which Liberals have fought for years, but he was not prepared to go to Parliament having signed away his liberty."[100]

The second apparent surprise was that Macarthur's name was not to appear on the ballot paper. Perhaps mischievously a local paper had already flagged up the difficulty the week before by asking "will she have to be nominated in her proper name of Mrs Anderson?" and "Is it a proper thing that candidates for the House of Commons should be allowed to seek election under a name that they are not legally entitled

---

99   Kenneth Brown, Baker, and Son. 'Miss Macarthur And The Women's Party'. *Times* [London, England] 13 Sept. 1918: 8. *The Times Digital Archive*. Web. 21 July 2015.

100 'Triangular Contest At Stourbridge'. *Times* [London, England] 29 Nov. 1918: 10. *The Times Digital Archive*. Web. 21 July 2015.

to use?"[101] The very same week she started to add in brackets under her chosen name "Mrs. W.C. Anderson" on all propaganda. When she handed in her nomination paper, to her "complete surprise", according to Hamilton, they were rejected by the returning officer who ruled that she must go before the electors under her married name as Anderson. She had taken legal opinion and her friend Violet Markham, who was married to Mr Carruthers, was nominated without any trouble in Mansfield, Nottinghamshire.[102] Even the Unionist *Daily Express* remarked that if "Our Mary" was the name on the ballot paper her victory would have been a certainty.[103]

The version of events which had appeared in the local newspaper two days later was slightly different. Macarthur arrived at the returning officer at Oldbury council buildings with a set of papers in which she described herself as "Mary Reid Macarthur, married woman, wife of William Crawford Anderson, journalist." The returning officer declared the nomination invalid on the grounds that the description was insufficient. Macarthur argued the point but to no avail whereupon she produced another nomination paper describing her as "Mary Reid Anderson, commonly called Mary Reid Macarthur, secretary."[104] Precisely what appeared on the ballot paper has proved impossible to discover. It is worth pointing out that the inclusion of party names is a comparatively recent innovation so the word "Labour" did not appear.

The election campaign had begun in earnest during the weekend of 24 November 1918. Both *The Weekly News* and the *County Express* carried

---

101 'Notes by the way', *The Weekly News* 29 November 1918. This was not the first time that the use of Macarthur's maiden name had been question. The London *Daily Mail* ran a paragraph headed "Why?" shortly after Anderson's election "Miss Macarthur … for some rather recondite reason, retains her maiden name, in connection, at all events with her public activities. An author or actress may do so for obvious reasons, but why the wife of a Labour leader?" *Daily Mail*, 16 January 1915.

102 Hamilton, ibid, pp176-177.

103 *Daily Express* 9 December 1918, quoted ibid p177.

104 'The General Elections … the Nominations', *The Weekly News* 6 December 1918.

front page advertisements from each of the candidates. Labour planned a meeting for the following Thursday at the Wesleyan Chapel, Brades Village, in Oldbury. Macarthur was listed in her maiden name and the advert signed off by saying "Women Specially Invited" and "Work is Worship". Wilson made it clear that he would continue to support the Coalition and that women electors were "Heartily Invited" to a meeting planned at Oldbury Town Hall the following Monday. *The Weekly News* reported that Macarthur had "taken up residence in the Talbot Hotel, Stourbridge", that she planned a meeting at the council school Warley and had set up a committee room in Church Street, Oldbury.[105] The following week she published her fourteen point programme on the front page of both local papers.[106] She opened by saying "My candidature is endorsed by the National Labour Party, and has the warm support of the National Federation of Women Workers." She sums up the objectives of the Labour Party as "To unite all who contribute to the Wealth and Welfare of the World by hand or by brain, to secure, not privileges for any section or class of the community, but a full share of the good things of life, material and spiritual, for all."

Before itemising her programme she answered the issue of her gender:

"I DO NOT APOLOGISE FOR MY SEX. It takes a man and a woman to make THE IDEAL HOME; and I believe they neither can build THE IDEAL WORLD without the help of the other. In the new Parliament, where laws affecting every household in the land will be framed, the point of view of THE MOTHER, AS WELL AS THE FATHER, should find expression.

"If I am returned to the House of Commons, I shall try to voice in a special sense the aspirations of THE WOMEN WORKERS OF THIS

---

105 Advertisement, *The Weekly News* 24 November 1918.

106 During the war President Wilson had promoted a 14 point manifesto for peace in Europe.

LAND, to whose cause I have been privileged to devote my life, and who, in every industrial centre in the United Kingdom and Ireland, are voluntarily contributing their pennies to the expense of my candidature.

"I shall also feel entitled to speak for the WOMAN WHOSE WORK NEVER ENDS – the woman in the home, who faces and solves every day a multitude of problems – the woman who has been too often neglected or forgotten by politicians, the mother of the children upon whom THE FUTURE PRIDE AND STRENGTH OF THE NATION DEPENDS.

"At the same time I shall not be deflected from my duties to my constituents, **MEN AND WOMEN**."

Much of what she says appears in the material published by other Labour Party candidates: she wanted "a people's permanent peace, the end of conscription, the speedy return of fighting men as their wives and children want them back", justice not charity for soldiers and sailors, the restoration of freedom, a living wage and no unemployment, the redemption of pledges, a million new homes, a fair system of taxation, public good before private profit, and the dignity of labour. She did make one point directed at women voters:

"A MAN'S PAY FOR A MAN'S WORK

It should be illegal to employ a woman on the same work as a man for less pay. The standard of life must not be lowered by unfair competition. THIS IS IN THE INTERESTS OF BOTH MEN AND WOMEN."[107]

Macarthur clearly saw Wilson as her main threat even though Fisher was to be the Coupon candidate. Wilson continued to insist that he would support the Coalition. Fisher made it clear he was the formal Coalition candidate, reproducing in full the "Coupon" letter from Lloyd George and Bonar Law at every opportunity. Macarthur expressed surprise that Fisher had been given the Coalition Coupon. "Mr. J. W. Wilson had

---

107 'The General Election 1918, From Miss Mary Macarthur (Mrs W.C. Anderson) To the Electors of the Stourbridge Parliamentary Division', *The Weekly News*, 29 November 1918 and election address leaflet.

the reputation of being an honourable man" but if he couldn't protect himself from "a smack in the face" by the Coalition he did not seem well qualified to protect his constituents from the Coalition Government. She then pointed out that one of the men giving prominent support to Wilson "was Major Green, who was an old enemy of hers, and she was not surprised to see him support Mr Wilson. When she first came to Cradley Heath Mr Green was one of the men she had to deal with in endeavouring to secure better wages for the women chain makers, who were making chains at a wage less than a penny an hour. When Mr. Wilson spoke last week he gave credit to the Coalition Government for the passing of the Wages Temporary Regulation Bill, which guaranteed that wages could not be reduced for six months unless an Arbitration Court decides it. She was amazed when she heard Mr. Wilson claim credit for the Bill, because the Bill was drafted by a committee of 16 trades unionists, and every clause in that Bill affecting women was drawn up by her personally."[108]

Macarthur, Wilson and Fisher traded points for the remainder of the contest. Wilson did not attack her on account of her sex, mainly focusing on refuting points about his voting record.[109] Fisher however, made personal attacks something of a hallmark of his campaign. He referred to Wilson as the Oldbury version of the Vicar of Bray and a "pious Asquithian pacifist", reminding his listeners that Wilson had originally been elected as a Unionist. His attacks on Macarthur were even more unpleasant but contained some references that could have been gender specific. Macarthur was the "cooing dove of blood red Bolshevism". He also attacked her through her husband, making what seems to have been an explicit sexual comment: a man was known by the company he kept and he "supposed that lady electors would agree

---

108 'Miss Mary Macarthur at Oldbury', *The Weekly News*, 29 November 1918.
109 'Mr J.W. Wilson Opens His Campaign', *The Weekly News*, 29 November 1918 and 'Mr Wilson at Rounds Green, A Reply to His Critics', *The Weekly News*, 13 December 1918.

that was a motto which would apply equally to their sex. He judged Miss Macarthur by the company she kept. In the first place her mate in life was that great statesman and worthy representative of the great steel city of England, Weary Willie Anderson of the I.L.P."[110] There is no evidence that Anderson was known as "Willie", always Will. Fisher differentiated between Wilson and Macarthur: whereas he could shake hands with Wilson, as he did on nomination day, "but he thought he would rather have his hand cut off than shake that of Miss Macarthur … if she were his own sister he could never forgive her because of the pacifist, defeatist party she and her political associates belonged to; the conscientious objectors and skulkers who fermented strikes when men in the trenches wanted munitions and the men on the high seas guns." At the same meeting Fisher's wife spoke on his behalf explaining that "She was in favour of parents not going to work when they were rearing children, and she was disgusted when she heard of Miss Macarthur trotting her child about as a canvasser."[111] Macarthur did use her daughter in the campaign. Hamilton reports "Her own Nancy, now three years old, figured largely in the campaign; a 'Message from wee Nancy' with a picture of the golden-haired earnest little face, reminded the electors that the Labour candidate stands for 'An equal chance for every child'."[112]

Commenting on the election, Hamilton, Macarthur's biographer, describes the nastiness of the campaign against Macarthur. It is "impossible to convey to the inexperienced what mud-slinging can do in the hands of a practised performer. To be a friend of Ramsey MacDonald and Philip Snowden unloosed the flood tides. In Stourbridge they flowed vigorously, although less violently than in Attercliffe … where Macarthur's husband, Anderson, was the defending Labour candidate.

---

110 'Mr. Victor Fisher Takes To The Field, Caustic Comments Upon His Opponents' Records', *The Weekly News*, 6 December 1918.

111 'Mr. Victor Fisher at Langley, The Need for a Strong Government', *The Weekly News*, 13 December 1918.

112 Hamilton, ibid p178.

"Thanks to the fairness of the local press in Stourbridge", which is now our main primary source, nearly a century later it is difficult to know what was said but Hamilton reports "on the platform and the doorstep she was a Bolshevik, a pacifist, a defeatist: a woman who had held up the supply of munitions and now refused to exact the just penalties of crime from the Hun. And so on. The fight in that respect was like others of the day."[113] But there were some bright spots: The Rev Halbert, the vicar of St Hilda's Warley Woods, gave Macarthur a ringing endorsement in his parish magazine speaking of the small number of women who can expect to be elected to Parliament, "I think it nothing less than a national loss if Mary Macarthur should not be one of that number."[114]

The result does deserve close attention as it is the only one with a woman candidate in the West Midlands for which we have a broadly comparable result from the second election in 1910:

1918 – Electorate 42,205 (including Stourbridge)				1910 – Electorate 18,200 (excluding Stourbridge)			
Candidate	Party	Votes	%	Candidate	Party	Votes	%
Wilson	Liberal	8920	38.5	Wilson	Liberal	7894	50.9
Macarthur	Labour	7587	32.7	Timmins	Unionist	7625	49.1
Fisher	NDLP	6690	28.8				
Majority			1333	5.8	Majority		269	1.7
Turnout			55.0	Turnout			85.3

Wilson's incumbency enabled him to retain his vote of 1910, even slightly increasing his majority, despite being a non-Coupon Liberal. Fisher, as a Unionist candidate in all but name, failed to match the previous Unionist vote. Macarthur clearly benefitted from the extension of the franchise.

Whether she would have won had her chosen name been on the ballot paper is open to question. Her biographer thought it impossible

---

113 Ibid, pp177-176.
114 'Election notes … Miss Mary Macarthur', *Evening Despatch*, Birmingham, 12 December 1918.

to calculate how many of those "simple souls" failed to realise that "Anderson" on the ballot paper stood for "Our Mary".[115] Macarthur herself clearly thought it an important factor. After the declaration of the result she thanked the returning officer for his work especially for the courteous way in which he had performed an unpleasant duty in a pleasant manner. Then she quoted Iago from Shakespeare's *Othello* "Who steals my purse steals trash; 'tis something, nothing ... But he that filches from me my good name ... Robs me of that which not enriches him, And makes me poor indeed." Mr Vernon and others may ask "what's in a name?"; the answer was votes. She then made one other comment about her two male opponents: in her view, the best man won. The returning officer responded to her by saying that he had taken the decision judicially, believing it was the right course for the right reason.[116]

The turnout of 54.96% was just below the average of 55.68% for the region.[117] To achieve parity with Wilson she would have required another 1,333 votes, meaning a substantially higher Labour vote and an above average turnout. Charles Stitch, the newly elected Labour MP for Kingswinford, believed that organisational problems had reduced the Labour vote, saying he had heard that Cradley had not played its part.[118] The failure of Labour to field a candidate for the 1922 election when the Unionists ousted Wilson, suggests that the local party was not particularly well established. However, Fisher's attacks, and Wilson's patriarchal incumbency, may have been important factors in Macarthur's defeat.

For both Macarthur and her husband the results were a bitter disappointment. Anderson lost Attercliffe, thought to be as safe as any seat could be. Macarthur came a good second in Stourbridge.

---

115 Hamilton, ibid, p177.
116 'The General Election', *The Weekly News* 3 January 1919.
117 The West Midlands as defined in Kinnear, ibid, map p145.
118 'Labour and the Coalition Government', *Dudley Herald*, 11 January 1919.

Macarthur's husband died of influenza complicated by pneumonia in February 1919.[119] Macarthur was reselected for the Stourbridge seat in January 1920 and undertook several campaign meetings.[120] She became unwell soon after and died on New Year's Day 1921,[121] coincidentally the same day that the National Federation of Women Workers formally amalgamated with the National Union of General Workers, the forerunner of today's GMB trade union.[122]

---

119 Hamilton, ibid p182.

120 Unheaded, *Worcester Chronicle*, 24 January 1920, 'Labour Meeting at Langley', *Midland Chronicle*, 30 January 1920.

121 Hamilton Ibid pp191-195. In 1922, Labour did not field a candidate for Stourbridge; Wilson lost the seat to the Conservatives and never stood again. Labour fielded Wilfred Wellock in 1923 and he came third with 9,050 votes. Wellock was a pacifist, and had been imprisoned as a conscientious objector during the First World War. He was an organic gardener, an admirer of Ghandi and a vegetarian. He came second in 1924 with 14,113 and eventually won a by-election in 1927 with 16,561. See book review by Jo Hunt, 'A life of peace – A biography of Wilfred Wellock' by Andrew Rigby, Bridport, in *The Black Countryman Vol 22 No 1*, Winter 1989 p63 and H. Jack Haden 'The Rise and Fall of an Idealist', *The Black Countryman Vol 23 No 2* , Spring 1990, p32. See also Wilfred Wellock biography on Spartacus Educational http://spartacus-educational.com/FWWwellockW.htm downloaded 20 August 2015. Wellock lost in 1931 to the Conservatives with Stourbridge returning to Labour in 1945, after which the constituency was dismembered. See Craig p503 entry 486. Victor Fisher went on to fight West Ham, Stratford, as a Conservative in 1924 coming second to Labour with just over a quarter of the vote. See Craig, ibid, p274 entry 260.

122 Hunt, C., *The National Federation of Women's Workers 1906-1921*, London, 2014, p175.

Chapter Four

Margery Corbett Ashby in Birmingham, Ladywood

IT was clearly seen as a coup when the Birmingham Liberal newspapers headlined the news that it was "A soldier's wife for Ladywood". This was illustrated with head and shoulders pictures of both Corbett Ashby and her husband in uniform, an army captain on active service with The Queens. Her father had been the Liberal MP for East Grinstead. She and her barrister husband had a small son born during the war. The paper commented that the Ladywood Liberals had secured "a candidate who combines a charming personality with eloquence and practical idealism. The occasion was felt to be both significant and memorable."[123] She was to take on Neville Chamberlain, son of Joseph, who went on, as Prime Minister, to lead Britain to war in 1939.

Corbett Ashby was supported at the Liberal Party adoption meeting by Mrs Osler of the Women's Suffrage Society, who it transpired, had

---

123 'A Soldier's Wife For Ladywood', *Birmingham Gazette*, 20 November 1918.

48

been the original choice as Liberal candidate.[124] Corbett Ashby was a Poor Law Guardian for one of London's biggest unions, Wandsworth, had extensive experience of social and public work, and in addition to taking the Classical Tripos at Cambridge, held a B.A. from Dublin University. She was for free trade, home rule for Ireland, perfect equality for "men and women, rather, equality for maids and wives and preference for mothers", equal pay for equal work, and more opportunities for women in trades and professions. She would support the Coalition if it were to bring in Liberal measures, but when it departed from those principles, she would be in hot opposition.[125]

Corbett Ashby did have her doubts. Whilst believing that women should be candidates and MPs, the invitation had come like a "bolt from the blue" and the "idea of fighting Neville Chamberlain in Birmingham, the stronghold of the Chamberlains and Tariffs, seemed absurd." She shared her misgivings with her colleagues in the National Union of Women Suffrage Societies, expecting them to find it amusing or meet resentment. Their reaction was very supportive and she made her way to Birmingham. She had found the election unpleasant. She concluded that being a woman was neither an advantage nor a disadvantage, "I found out that even one of my Liberal executive had cast his vote against me."[126]

There were domestic issues for Corbett Ashby, letters between her and her husband during the campaign sometimes made no reference to what was happening in Ladywood, but a real concern by both for their son Michael. Initially she stayed with Catherine Osler but later transferred to a small hotel. She then decided that the child should join

---

124 'Woman Candidate and the League of Nations', *Birmingham Post*, 27 November 1918.

125 'Ladywood's Lead, Birmingham's First Lady Candidate Adopted', *Evening Despatch*, Birmingham, 20 November 1918. 'Ladywood Division, Adoption of Lady Liberal Candidate' *Birmingham Post*, 20 November 1918.

126 Letter from husband to Margery Corbett Ashby, 2 December 1918 and letter from Margery Corbett Ashby, to husband, 5 December 1918. MICA/A30 General correspondence 1918, Women's Reading Room, London School of Economics.

her in Birmingham with care "being shared with her own mother and father and a nanny who arrived to support the campaign," she recalled.[127]

In one letter to her husband she confessed that she was "quite undecided until learning the election will be on December 14". She believed there were other better qualified candidates but felt bound to accept the invitation. She was concerned about their son but assured her husband that "I shan't be away very much as the constituency is a small industrial one quite easy to cover."[128] Her husband quickly and positively responded and she in turn said "Darling, your letter was an immense relief to me. I am so glad you don't think me a fool for standing!" She pointed out that she was standing against Neville, not Austen, Chamberlain adding "the man who was 1st class as mayor of Birmingham but an utter failure as Minister of National Service.[129] Still, of course, a very strong local candidate, as you say not really a fair seat … my folk are apparently pleased with me … I am afraid that the ILP candidate's folk will feel sore but he [Kneeshaw, the Labour candidate] isn't in the least representative of the general moderate Liberal or even Labour opinion … Out of work pay begins on Monday and hundreds of women who have been discharged will not be eligible. Into this cauldron Ll G [Lloyd George] plunges a general election and instead of a Coalition of Liberal and Labour which would have checked Labour, has a Unionist lion and Liberal lamb lying down together and Labour in opposition. I feel heartbroken over it all."[130]

Corbett Ashby campaigned hard on the basis that as a woman she could represent women, but also men. Her leaflets were invariably

---

127 Margery Corbett Ashby, *Memoirs*, Horsted Keynes, 1996, p96-98.

128 Letter from Margery Corbett Ashby to husband, 20 November 1918, MICA/B6, 1918 General Election, Women's Reading Room, London School of Economics.

129 In 1916, Lloyd George appointed Neville Chamberlain "director-general of the department of national service, but disagreements between them led Chamberlain to resign." BBC History Page http://www.bbc.co.uk/history/historic_figures/ chamberlain_arthur_neville.shtml, downloaded 11 September 2017.

130 Letter from Margery Corbett Ashby to husband, 22 November 1918, MICA/B6, 1918 General Election, Women's Reading Room, London School of Economics.

headed "A soldier's wife for Ladywood" and featured a picture of her with her son. Her election address included a paragraph calling for equality before the law between men and women in questions of marriage, morals and the home, opportunities for technical training, equal pay for equal work above a sound minimum, and access to all trade, industries and professions.[131]

The new Ladywood constituency had been carved out of the former West Birmingham constituency which had long been represented by Joseph Chamberlain, father of the new candidate Neville Chamberlain, and the former Central division which, for many years, had been the base of the radical John Bright. Neville Chamberlain revealed to the new Ladywood that he had refused several offers to stand elsewhere in Birmingham.[132]

The public response of Neville Chamberlain to Corbett Ashby was one of disdain. He told the electorate that "You really ought to be extremely flattered. I am told that Mrs Ashby is a charming and accomplished lady, and has taken the trouble to come all the way from her country house in Sussex in order to represent an urban constituency."[133]

However, others believed that she was making an impact: "Reports from the division suggest that the electors are showing their appreciation of the honour. Mrs Corbett Ashby's charming personality, coupled with her quickness in grasping and effectively answering all sorts of questions, is telling strongly. An encouraging feature of the recent meetings has been not merely the number of women present, but the proportion of women voters who have been obviously impressed by Mrs Ashby's sincerity and experience of the everyday needs and aspirations of working women." It was also evident that as a soldier's wife she shared

---

131 Assorted leaflets and election address in file MICA/B6, 1918 General Election, Women's Reading Room, London School of Economics.

132 'Mr N. Chamberlain as a Coalitionist, Candidate for Ladywood Division...' *Birmingham Post*, 22 November 1918.

133 'Occasional notes', *Evening Despatch*, Birmingham, 29 November 1918.

the daily anxiety of other women who had sons and husbands on active service.[134]

The real battle in Ladywood was between the Unionists and the Labour Candidate, Councillor J. W. Kneeshaw, who represented Rotton Park on the City Council. He had been nominated as a Labour Parliamentary candidate for the former West Birmingham division in 1914, expected within the following 12 months but never held due to the outbreak of war. Then aged 35 he was described as a "man of enormous vitality" whose early life had been marred by the spectre of poverty. He was originally from Yorkshire and had moved to Birmingham in search of work ten years before and rapidly rose through the local Labour movement. Having walked around the country in search of work he was well aware of the "tramp problem", having himself stayed in doss-houses and slept in the open air. He had won Rotton Park in 1911 with a majority of 12 which he increased to 599 a year later, due, it was believed, to him winning Liberal support.[135] Chamberlain quickly took up the theme of Kneeshaw's opposition to the war making it a main plank of his campaign saying "it was a slander that such a man should claim to represent the electors of that division and an outrage on a patriotic city to be asked to support him."[136]

When nominations closed, Corbett Ashby was one of nine Liberal candidates across Birmingham and was featured in a front page promotional box in the Liberal *Evening Despatch*. Corbett Ashby's occupation was described as "married woman". The local press reported that there were 29,465 men voters and 12,865 women voters,[137] with

---

134 'Election Progress, Latest Reports From The Constituencies', *Evening Despatch*, Birmingham, 29 November, 1918.

135 'Labour's Choice of Candidate, Next Election in West Birmingham', *Evening Despatch*, Birmingham, 10 January 1914.

136 'Ladywood Division, Ald. Chamberlain on the So-called Representative of Labour' *Birmingham Post*, 27 November, 1918.

137 'Nomination day, The Birmingham Divisions' and 'Nine for Birmingham' *Evening Despatch*, 4 December 1918.

6,516 absent voters, mainly on active service.[138] The contest between Kneeshaw and Chamberlain became very acrimonious. Each had their meetings disrupted by rival hecklers and there was a determined attempt to get Liberal voters to back the Coalition.[139] Corbett Ashby made some headway on the conscription issue. Chamberlain would not commit himself on whether he would support or oppose conscription. She made it clear she would oppose and "received the benediction" of the Ladywood branch of the Discharged Soldiers' Federation,[140] who went so far as to publish their own leaflet in her support.[141] Corbett Ashby was busy with lunchtime open air meetings, often accompanied by her mother and father. Mrs Osler was writing to men voters on her behalf suggesting that they should support Corbett Ashby.[142] At one meeting Corbett Ashby identified housing as the main issue that was uppermost in the minds of voters. She asked them to vote for her as she cared about housing.

A vote for the Coalition was a vote for a Conservative majority who would not provide a solution to the housing crisis.[143] Towards the end of the campaign she was accompanied by her husband, Captain Ashby, but he could not actually attend meetings because he was in uniform; however his arrival in Birmingham made front page news.[144] There was one section of the community who would not be voting for her: the

---

138 'The Election, 56,000 Out of 68,000 papers sent', *Evening Despatch*, Birmingham, 6 December 1918.

139 'Birmingham's absent voters … A severe heckling' *Evening Despatch*, 5 December, 1918.

140 'The Election … Ladywood', *Evening Despatch*, Birmingham, 6 December 1918.

141 "A soldier's wife for Ladywood" Quarto leaflet, printed and published by Hudson and Son, Livery Street. (Official Liberal Party material was printed by Templar, Edmund Street), file 7MCA/B/06 1918 General Election, Women's Reading Room, London School of Economics.

142 'The Secret Ballot … Ladywood', *Evening Despatch*, Birmingham, 9 December 1918.

143 'Coalition majority is a Tory Majority, Mrs Corbett Ashby's Fact for Ladywood Electors', *Evening Despatch*, Birmingham, 11 December 1918.

144 'Election Issues crystallising … Mrs Ashby Gives Facts to Ladywood', *Evening Despatch*, Birmingham, 12 December 1918.

executive committee of the Birmingham branch of the United Irish League, recommended Kneeshaw.[145]

The Unionist *Evening Mail* carried a "sketch" of the contest in Ladywood. It again highlighted the "contrast" between Kneeshaw and Chamberlain during the war. Chamberlain, though being above military age, "assisted the national cause to the utmost of his power, sacrificing his time, money, and his energy without stint." Kneeshaw "has done exactly the opposite. He has decried his country; declared that our objects are the same as Germany's; served with the little crowd of anti-English men who have worked all through against our cause, refused to fight himself, although of military age, and tried to prevent others being called up for service; preached pacifism and advocated peace by negotiation instead of peace by victory." Chamberlain was the son of one of Birmingham's greatest citizens whereas Kneeshaw was a bricklayer and "probably a very good bricklayer". The writer's sarcasm is turned on Corbett Ashby almost as a deliberate afterthought and repeated Chamberlain's line that she was a stranger to the city, "one may be excused for almost overlooking that there is a third (candidate) – a lady." There is a short biography and then the comment "Beyond this, we regret to say we know little or nothing about the lady. She is almost a stranger to Birmingham, and after she has flitted fitfully across the stage of this electoral contest, will no doubt vanish back into the unknown."[146] It is perhaps significant that this was the only newspaper cutting of the election campaign which survived to become part of the Neville Chamberlain archive.[147]

Chamberlain did react to the opposition woman candidate. He held two meetings specifically for women voters. One was convened on an

---

145 'Election Notes and Points … the Irish Vote', *Evening Despatch*, Birmingham, 10 December 1918.

146 'Mr. Neville Chamberlain and Mr. Kneeshaw, a contrast in Ladywood', *Evening Mail*, Birmingham, 5 December 1918.

147 Papers of Neville Chamberlain, Elections, Municipal and National 1911-1935, NC 5/12/11 Cadbury Research Library University of Birmingham.

afternoon because they assumed women would find it difficult to attend evening meetings. Women had shown the whole country what they could do during the war and they had been given the vote in recognition of that splendid work and must realise the power placed in their hands: "Politics concerned the government of the country, and if the country were poorly governed in the future, it would be as much the fault of the women as the men," before outlining a series of social reforms that he would support.[148] Chamberlain also issued a special duplicated leaflet headed "A word to the Ladies!" With the salutation "Dear Madam" he urged women to vote wisely, reminded them of his record in supporting child care when Lord Mayor, how he wanted to give help to mothers, especially widows, so their children did not have to go into institutions and wanted to build more houses urging women to "remember that an attractive home means a contented husband."[149] In his printed election address Chamberlain qualifies his pledges to provide assistance to mothers saying that it would "only be given where parents recognise their responsibilities, and carry them out to the best of their ability."[150] It does appear that Chamberlain's special meeting for women and the leaflet for women voters, were the only propaganda specifically produced for women by the Unionists in the City. Significantly, given the proximity of Ladywood and Smethwick, Christabel Pankhurst was not asked to cross the boundary to support Chamberlain against his pacifist and woman opponents. Before polling day Chamberlain was reported to be "confident of victory".[151]

---

148 'Women Voters. Mr Neville Chamberlain and Their Position in Politics…', *Evening Mail*, Birmingham, 12 December 1918.

149 Papers of Neville Chamberlain, 'Elections, Municipal and National 1911-1935', NC 5/12/8 Cadbury Research Library University of Birmingham.

150 Papers of Neville Chamberlain, 'Elections, Municipal and National 1911-1935', NC 5/12/9 Cadbury Research Library University of Birmingham.

151 'Ladywood Division, Mr. Neville Chamberlain Confident of Victory', *Birmingham Post*, 14 December 1918.

On the eve of the election, presumably with her consent as she was sent a page proof which survives in her files, an *Evening Despatch* full front page for distribution in Ladywood was headed "Vote for Mrs Corbett Ashby: A soldier's wife for Ladywood". A page lead article was headed "Mrs Corbett Ashby and Little Michael". It was very much a "human interest" piece, by-lined "a Ladywood Journalist" that gave her the opportunity of speaking about her education, the appalling housing conditions she had encountered in Ladywood, the difficulties that the electorate had in even recalling the name of their previous MP, her family's war record, and the joy she had caring for a small child.[152]

On polling day Corbett Ashby toured her committee rooms and it was reported that she was looking remarkably well despite her heavy schedule of the previous weeks. The polling stations had been quiet and there was a feeling that women were very reluctant to vote, with one campaign worker commenting that "It's like trying to get some of them into a dentist." Some went to the door, paused and then waited for a neighbour to join them before going in together. One woman turned up at a committee room just after 8 a.m. and asked where she should vote saying "I want to make sure of my vote getting in for that lady before I start work."[153]

The *Evening Mail* ran a small post-election review of the new women voters across the city noting that voting among women varied considerably. In residential districts, such as Edgbaston and Moseley, the number of women voting was large, in fact more than were expected. Some women refused to vote unless they were accompanied by their

---

152 Page pull proof of *Evening Despatch*, Birmingham, 13 December 1918 in file MICA/B6, 1918 General Election, Women's Reading Room, London School of Economics. Future researchers should note that this edition of the *Despatch* is not included in the micro-fiche film created by the British Library and held at Birmingham Library. The copy of the page proof and final paper held by LSE are probably the only copies now available.

153 Rush election in progress … .Ladywood', *Evening Despatch*, Birmingham, 14 December 1918.

husbands. "It was noteworthy that when the ladies received their papers from the presiding officer they became serious and business-like, and generally speaking, were most careful not to let their husbands decide against whose name they placed their cross ... In some working class areas districts – of which Aston is an example – the number of women voters in the earlier hours was negligible. A prominent worker declared that during his perambulations he had not seen one woman voter ... One point worth noting, is that the great loyalty which the women members of the Co-operative and Non-conformists are showing towards their nominees who are generally Liberals, but in one instance at least, Labour ... it cannot be denied that in the divisions generally the bulk of election work done by women is being done by members of Labour, Socialistic and Liberal organisations."[154]

Chamberlain was certain that he had won. In a diary entry dated the 15 December, he recorded that he had spoken at 18 meetings in the constituency and eight times for other candidates. "Hustings well attended as mine is considered the most 'interesting' in the city. Annie [his wife] splendid in enthusing workers. Believe I have won easily but result will not be known till the 28th."[155]

During the campaign Chamberlain kept his sisters up to date with the election in a series of regular letters. He clearly did not like Kneeshaw and commented on Corbett Ashby and her campaign. On 16 November he tells Ida "Leo Amery [his agent] is here and we talk electioneering all the time. Between you and me I loathe the business and I am by no means looking forward to the next few weeks. So far there is no opposition to Austen [his brother who was returned unopposed for Birmingham West] but I see tonight that I am to have a lady (a Mrs Corbett Ashby from East Grinstead) as the "official" Liberal candidate

---

154 'Birmingham Scenes, Many Women Among The Voters, One Over 90 at Duddeston', *Evening Mail*, Birmingham, 14 December 1918.

155 Diary of Neville Chamberlain 1913-1922, NC2/20 Cadbury Research Library University of Birmingham.

from East Grinstead. I presume this means she is an Asquithian but anyway I should think she is quite likely to lose her £150 deposit."[156] The following week, on 1 December he sent Ida a detailed update on the campaign conceding "It is much too early to try to say what will be the result but I think I can safely prophesy that the lady (Mrs Corbett Ashby) won't go very far. Kneeshaw is rather an unknown quantity ...".[157] A different tone emerged in a letter to Hilda on 9 December. His team had looked at the canvass returns and whilst they were certain that Kneeshaw had no chance they noted that "Mrs Ashby is getting a lot of support among the women. Of course they are of a doubtful quality but if the result is that the lady comes out second and K at that bottom that will not be unsatisfactory ... ".[158] As the polls closed on 14 December Chamberlain again wrote to Ida mentioning that "we had two women's meetings. They were sparsely attended but I think were useful and Annie (his wife) addressed each of them most effectively." Of Ashby Corbett he said "I hear that her supporters began with great enthusiasm and high hopes but they have gradually become more depressed and hopeless." His prediction of the result was Chamberlain 8000, Kneeshaw 3000, with Corbett Ashby 2000, on a 50% poll.[159] The accuracy of the prediction, given a margin of error, demonstrates the effectiveness of the Unionist election machine.

The result was declared on Saturday 28 December. All newspapers took an interest in the outcome of the votes for women across the country, publishing a "league table" of the defeated women candidates and showing their popular vote. The low turnout and lack of interest in

156 Papers of Neville Chamberlain, 'Letters to Ida and Hilda Chamberlain 1918', NC 18/1/191 Cadbury Research Library University of Birmingham.

157 Papers of Neville Chamberlain, 'Letters to Ida and Hilda Chamberlain 1918', NC 18/1/192 Cadbury Research Library University of Birmingham.

158 Papers of Neville Chamberlain, 'Letters to Ida and Hilda Chamberlain 1918', NC 18/1/193 Cadbury Research Library University of Birmingham.

159 Papers of Neville Chamberlain, 'Letters to Ida and Hilda Chamberlain 1918', NC 18/1/194 Cadbury Research Library University of Birmingham.

the election in Birmingham was noted, one paper saying "The 'peace' election in Birmingham justified its description. It was so peaceful as to be apathetic, and there were none of the more or less riotous scenes to which former elections have accustomed us. Perhaps the only excited people were the candidates themselves."[160]

Corbett Ashby did badly on a generally poor performance for non-Coupon Liberals. She polled less than one eighth of the votes and so lost her £150 deposit:

Candidate	Party	Votes	%
Chamberlain	Coalition Unionist	9405	69.5
Kneeshaw	Labour (ILP)	2572	19.0
Corbett Ashby	Liberal	1552	11.5
Turnout			50.5

Final electorate: Male voters – 20,465; Women voters – 12,865

Corbett Ashby's comments after the result reflected her Liberalism rather than her gender, saying that she believed the Coalition had won temporarily, because the mass of people were wishful that those in power when the Armistice was signed should finish the job.[161] Chamberlain wrote to his sister Ida saying that "the election has fairly finished the Liberals".[162] Labour generally did better than Liberals across the city but it was noted that Kneeshaw recorded the lowest vote among the eight Labour candidates who stood in Birmingham.[163] The Liberals only contested Ladywood once more, in the eight General Elections

---

160 'Midland Declaration Scenes … Quietest Election on Record', *Birmingham Gazette*, 30 December 1918.

161 'Duty of Liberals, Candidates Views on Causes of Defeat' *Birmingham Gazette*, 30 December 1918.

162 Papers of Neville Chamberlain, 'Letters to Ida and Hilda Chamberlain 1918', NC 18/1/195, 194 Cadbury Research Library University of Birmingham.

163 'How Birmingham Voted. Coalition's Huge Surplus of Votes', *Birmingham Post*, 31 December 1918.

between 1918 and 1945 and that was in 1924.[164] Indeed, they gradually withdrew from most seats in the city reaching a low point in 1935 when they contested none of the seats, with a slight recovery in 1945 when they contested four.[165] Corbett Ashby went on to fight seven more Parliamentary elections without success and conceded after the 1922 election that "Fighting as Liberal candidate in Richmond was much easier than fighting Birmingham."[166]

Whilst Corbett Ashby, like other women candidates, attracted media attention and possibly created additional interest in the constituency, she was squeezed with other non-Coupon Liberal candidates between a dominant Unionist machine and a Labour Party moving in on the Liberals' remaining working class support in Birmingham.

---

164 The Liberal intervention in 1924 probably saved Chamberlain's political career: without a Liberal in a three way fight he would possibly been defeated. In the subsequent two fights his majority was eroded in 1922, down to 2443, and in 1923 down to 1554. In 1924 with a Liberal taking 539 votes he scrapped home with a majority of 77 against the Labour candidate, Oswald Mosley. Labour took Ladywood in 1929 with a majority of 11, but Chamberlain was not the defeated Unionist, he had moved to neighbouring Edgbaston where he inherited a comfortable majority of over 14000.

165 Craig, ibid pp79-91, entries 73-85.

166 Handwritten note by Corbett Ashby headed 'Richmond Election 1922', MICA/B7, 1922 General Election, Women's Reading Room, London School of Economics.

Chapter Five

Conclusion

THE outcome of the 1918 election set the tone for the selection of future women candidates. It explains why so few stood in future years – in 1922 there were 33 women candidates, by 1929, 69; 1945, 87 and in 1959, 81.[167] None of the three 1918 pioneers stood again in the West Midlands. Just eight women stood in any of the twenty-four seats serving the region over the six elections from 1922 to 1935.[168] The first woman MP to take a seat in the House of Commons, was Nancy Astor, a Conservative, who "inherited" her Plymouth Sutton seat from a husband elevated to the peerage.[169] She was followed in 1921 by Margaret Witherington, a Liberal, for Louth who stood in place of her late husband Tom.[170] During the interwar years women MPs never numbered more than 15.[171] In the West Midlands region as

---

167 Brookes, ibid, pp40, 97, 149, 215.

168 Craig, ibid. West Midlands as defined by Kinnear ibid. The other interwar West Midlands women candidates were Hornabrook (Deritend, Liberal, 1929), Barton (King's Norton, Lab/Co-op, 1922 and 1923), Cadbury (Liberal 1923), Clarkson (Moseley, Liberal, 1923), Ward (Cannock, Conservative 1931 – elected, and 1935), Cooper (Walsall, Conservative, 1922), Stephen (Kidderminster, Labour, 1931) and Marshall (Smethwick, Liberal, 1929). See note below for women MPs in the interwar period for the modern West Midlands region.

169 Brookes, ibid, p17.

170 Brookes, ibid, p28.

171 Craig quoted Butler, D., *British Political Facts 1900-1985*, London, 1964, Sixth edition, 1986, p249.

presently defined, there were just four women MPs, all serving for just one term.[172]

The most important conclusion to be drawn from 1918 is that women candidates did not bring a gender bonus. Women voters did not necessarily vote for women candidates. Had that been the case, Pankhurst, Macarthur and Corbett Ashby would have won easily:

Constituency	Candidate	Women Voters	Votes cast for women candidate	Votes for winning male candidate
Birmingham Ladywood	Corbett Ashby	12,865	1,552	9,405
Smethwick	Pankhurst	12,726	8,614	9,389
Stourbridge	Macarthur	16,699	7,587	8,920

A study of the 1918 election based on material in Plymouth argues that a gendered language of patriotism was successfully deployed by the Coalition in opposition to a fracturing language of class and gender. No attempt was made to develop new policies around consumer and food issues, but rather focussed on women's relationship with the war, which was constructed in terms of their relationship with men fighting the war. They were urged to cast their votes as proxies for their absent husbands, brothers or sons,[173] which would have meant in most constituencies voting for men. However, where the "rhetoric of patriotism" coincided with a woman candidate in Smethwick it's clear that women voters did not vote on those lines in great enough numbers. Party label was paramount and women in Stourbridge, Smethwick and Ladywood opted for party rather than gender.

---

172 Brookes, ibid, pp271-278: Lady Cynthia Mosley, (Stoke-on-Trent, Labour, 1929-1931); Miss Edith Picton-Turberville, (The Wrekin, Labour, 1929-1931); Mrs Ida Copeland, (Stoke-on-Trent, Conservative, 1931-1935); Mrs Sarah Ward, (Cannock, Conservative, 1931-1935).

173 Hilson, M., "Women Voters and the Rhetoric of Patriotism in the British General Election of 1918" *Women's History Review*, London, 2006.

Nor did a woman candidate encourage more people to vote. Turnout out across the then United Kingdom was just 58.9%.[174] In the West Midlands, even with comparatively well-known candidates such as Macarthur and Pankhurst, the turn-out was lower than the national average with Stourbridge at 54.96%, Smethwick at 54.71%, and Birmingham Ladywood at 40.60%.[175] None quite matched the average turnout in the twenty-three contested seats in the West Midlands at 55.68%.[176/177]

Women candidates intensified interest in the otherwise lacklustre election. One journalist explained "When a woman enters the lists the novelty of the situation and the freshness of her point of view contrive to banish indifference and apathy."[178] This was certainly the case in the West Midlands. Chamberlain himself admitted to his sister that his contest in Ladywood was seen as the "most interesting" in the city, mainly because of Corbett Ashby's candidature. Pankhurst, and to a lesser extent Macarthur, attracted much more attention from the national and local press than any other challenging male candidates in the region, even those men that subsequently gained their seats. Whilst helpful with recognition it also meant additional scrutiny by both press and public, something which both Pankhurst and Macarthur, on occasions, found difficult.

---

174 As a control to discount Ireland which had special issues, Scotland where only one woman stood and Wales where no women stood in a constituency, a randomised sample of 12 English Borough and County seats provided a turnout of 58.95%.

175 Figures calculated from *The Times Guide to the House of Commons 1919*.

176 The West Midlands as defined in Kinnear ibid map page 145.

177 Mary Macarthur carried out an exercise which enables us to understand the difficulty of communicating with the absent voters on active service. She revealed, just a week before polling day, that she had written to the 6,000 absent voters using the regular postal service rather than relying on the free post available to candidates. Undelivered free post letters were not returned to the sender, however those with a stamp were. Over 3,000 were returned to Macarthur. See '3,000 out of 6,000 letters returned, Miss Macarthur's Absent Voter Revelation' *Evening Despatch*, Birmingham, 9 December 1918.

178 Brookes, ibid, p12.

Pankhurst, Macarthur and Corbett Ashby were not first choice candidates for their constituencies. Macarthur was a second choice as Labour candidate after a previously selected candidate had stood down, the Unionists had selected Thompson, and it emerged during the campaign that Corbett Ashby was selected because another potential candidate had dropped out. None of the parties had really thought through the possibility of fielding women candidates in winnable seats and those that ran were selected for what was left. This was compounded by organisational difficulties in Stourbridge, the use of an imported team in Smethwick, and a Liberal machine that had been destroyed by Joseph Chamberlain's creation of the Liberal Unionists. It should also be added that none of the women, even Macarthur, were truly local, enabling them to be portrayed as outsiders taking on well established locally respected men, all local patriarchs. Subsequent elections demonstrate that the respective parties were weak in both Stourbridge and Ladywood. Had the Unionists contested Smethwick in 1918, or Pankhurst had unequivocally stood as a Unionist, with a Coalition Coupon, the outcome may have been different.

Issues of child care still have an impact on women candidates today. It was no different in 1918. Two of the women candidates each had a small child and both children were photographed on election material. The letters between Corbett Ashby and her husband show a concern for the welfare of their child; doubtless similar discussions took place between Macarthur and her husband. In order to fight the election both stayed in hotels or were guests in other people's homes. We know that both Corbett Ashby and Macarthur had servants who could assist with childcare;[179] however, it highlights the additional stress and costs women candidates may incur. Additionally, Macarthur's alleged use of her child during canvass sessions was used to discredit her as a candidate and a mother.

---

179 Hamilton, ibid, pp126, 127 and 183.

By 1962 a woman MP reflected on her first period in Parliament during Clement Attlee's post war premiership saying "There was a Labour Government and the women MPs, with one exception, were all Labour women who had borne the brunt of long battles, many defeats, much victimisation and bitterness towards us as today would hardly be believed. And when success did come to the Party, there was the difficulty of the selection conference. Top organisers of both parties wrote off ten per cent of the votes cast if a woman was selected. Thus, many were called but few chosen, especially for 'safe' seats."[180] There is no evidence from 1918 to suggest that women candidates were rejected once nominated on the basis of their gender, with electorates preferring to vote according to party. There is abundant evidence to show that even at this early stage very little effort was made to place women into "winnable" seats. Lloyd George's note to Bonar Law supporting Pankhurst, almost casually, says "I am not sure we have any women candidates and think it highly desirable that we should."

Sadly, the experience of women in 1918, including those who stood in the West Midlands, was repeated for many years to come, and explains why in 2015 there were just 148 women elected to the House of Commons. Women candidates are not an issue with the electorate, the problem was, and is, their selection to seats where their party stands a chance of winning.

---

180 Mann, J. *Women in Parliament*, London, 1962, p11.

Bibliography and sources

Sources

The main primary sources are the very detailed contemporary reports which appeared in local newspapers. In the case of the Smethwick and Stourbridge constituencies this is mainly using material from the *Smethwick Telephone*, *The Weekly News*, and the *County Express*. The articles seem to be a mixture of submitted material and staff reports. The *Telephone* and *County Express* tended to focus on straight reporting, whereas *The Weekly News* often included editorial comments – sometimes mischievous. There is some evidence that these newspapers may have censored offensive references made during the campaigns, particularly in Stourbridge. In Birmingham, there were four daily newspapers covering the nine constituencies, all of which were partisan on behalf of the Unionist or Liberal cause. Whilst the Ladywood contest had added interest because of the participation of a woman candidate, the main contest between Labour and Unionist dominated the coverage. The women candidates, especially Pankhurst, attracted coverage in London based national newspapers such as *The Times* and the *Daily Mail*, whose proprietor, Lord Northcliffe, had privately promised to support a Pankhurst candidature. Reports in both papers tended to uncritically report the Pankhurst story.

Cuttings from other newspapers have been used and these were mainly found in the David Mitchell collection at the Museum of London and the Gertrude Tuckwell collection in the Trades Union Congress archives held at the London Metropolitan University. A contemporary book of cuttings by the Birmingham Library drew most of its material from the Unionist newspapers. Additional material, including reprints of articles favourable to Pankhurst was found in *Britannia*, the newspaper of the Women's Party. The use of any contemporary collection of newspaper cuttings should factor in the bias of the compiler and the availability of material at the time.

Each of the candidates published their memories of the campaign, though Pankhurst said least. Macarthur wrote a report for *The Woman Worker* and Corbett Ashby mentioned the campaign in her memoirs. Following Macarthur's death, Mary Hamilton published an account of the election in a sympathetic biography, some of which contradicted Macarthur's own immediate, and positive, reflections. The Cadbury Research Centre at Birmingham University holds a collection of Neville Chamberlain's personal correspondence, including letters to his sisters which mention his campaign. The Women's Collection at the London School of Economics holds Corbett Ashby's letters to her husband just after she had been selected. None of these were written for publication and therefore provide the most intimate thoughts from two candidates fighting the same election.

Some original election material has survived; much of it was reproduced word for word in the local newspapers. Mary Macarthur's election address is in the Gertrude Tuckwell collection. Christabel Pankhurst's is in the David Mitchell collection and Corbett Ashby's both at the LSE and Birmingham Library. The Birmingham Library also hold a copy of the election address for the Labour candidate in Ladywood and the Neville Chamberlain papers at the Cadbury Research Centre include his 1918 election address.

No original material for the other candidates in either Stourbridge or Smethwick has survived.

Reference books such as *The Times Guide to the House of Commons*, *Butler's Political Facts* and Craig's *British Parliamentary Election Results* proved invaluable. A wide range of secondary sources have been consulted and used, but it must be acknowledged that many were written from a particular perspective, mainly in the case of the Pankhurst candidacy, dependent on material curated by Pankhurst herself in *Britannia*. A literature search found just one paper on the Smethwick contest, in the *Women's History Review*, using Pankhurst's material, which came to conclusions not supported by any local research. Where possible all secondary sources have been checked for accuracy.

Periodicals

The following were systematically researched for the period of the 1918 election campaign.

> *Birmingham Gazette*, Birmingham
> *Birmingham Post*, Birmingham
> *Britannia*, London
> *County Express*, Stourbridge
> *Daily Mail*, London
> *Evening Mail*, Birmingham
> *Evening Gazette*, Birmingham
> *Evening Despatch*, Birmingham
> *Smethwick Telephone*, Birmingham
> *The Times*, London
> *The Weekly News*, Oldbury and Smethwick
> *Woman Worker*, London

References to other periodicals were either reprints appearing elsewhere or were taken from cuttings collections.

Archives

The Library of Birmingham, the collections of press cuttings and election addresses for 1918

David Mitchell collection at the Museum of London

Dudley Metropolitan Borough archives and local history centre

Cadbury Collection at the University of Birmingham, the papers of Neville and Austen Chamberlain

Sandwell Metropolitan Borough archives and local history centre

Trades Union Congress archives at the London Metropolitan University, papers of the National Federation of Women Workers and the Gertrude Tuckwell Collection

Women's Library at the London School of Economics, the papers of Margery Corbett Ashby

Books and academic articles quoted or consulted

Barnsley, George J., *Socialism in Birmingham and the Black Country 1850-1939*, Wolverhampton, 1998.

Barnsley, Tony, *Breaking Their Chains, Mary Macarthur and the Chainmakers' Strike of 1910*, London, 2010.

Brookes, Pamela, *Women at Westminster*, London, 1967.

Butler, David and Butler, Gareth, *British Political Facts 1900-1985*, 6th Edition, 1986.

Cawood, Ian, *The Liberal Unionist Party*, London 2012.

Christiansen, Rex, *A Regional History of the Railways of Great Britain, Volume 7, The West Midlands*, first published, 1973, 3rd revised edition Nairn 1991.

Corbett Ashby, Margery, *Memoirs*, Horsted Keynes, 1996.

Craig, F.W.S., *British Parliamentary Election Results 1918-1949*, Glasgow, 1969.

Doyle, Barry M., "Who Paid the Price of Patriotism? The Funding of Charles Stanton during the Merthyr Borough By-Election of 1915", *The English Historical Review*, Vol 109, No 434 (Nov 1994).

Ed Eustace, Claire, et al, *A Suffrage Reader, Charting Directions in British Suffrage History*, London, 2000.

Graves, Pamela M., *Labour Women, Women in British Working Class Politics 1918-1939*, Cambridge, 1994.

Gullace, Nicolette, "Christabel Pankhurst and the Smethwick Election: right wing feminism, the Great War and the ideology of consumption", *Women's History Review*, 23:3, p330-346, London, 2014.

Hamilton, Mary Agnes, *Margaret Bondfield*, London, 1924.

Hamilton, Mary Agnes, *Mary Macarthur, A biographical sketch*, London, 1925.

Harrison, Brian, *Separate Spheres, The Opposition to Women's Suffrage in Britain*, London, 1978.

Hilson, Mary, "Women Voters and the Rhetoric of Patriotism in the British General Election of 1918" *Women's History Review*, London, 2006.

How-Martyn, Edith, on behalf of Women's Election Committee, *The Need for Women Members of Parliament*, London, undated, but with a handwritten note in the copy held in the Museum of London "c.1922".

Hunt, Cathy, *The National Federation of Women's Workers 1906-1921*, London, 2014.

Inslip, K.W., *Smethwick from Hamlet to County Borough, a brief history*, Smethwick, 1966.

Keen, Richard, for House of Commons Library, *Women in Parliament and Government*, SN01250, London, 23 March 2015.

Kinnear, M, *The British Voter, an atlas and survey since 1885*, London, 1968.

Kelly's Directory for Warwickshire and Worcestershire, 1916, London, 1916.

Kelly's Directory of the Counties of Stafford, Warwick, and Worcester, London, 1924.

Kelly's Directory for Birmingham and suburbs 1916, London, 1916.

Keynes, John Maynard, *The Economic Consequences of Peace*, 1919, republished Lanham: Start Classics, 2014. Ebook Library.

Mann, Jean, *Woman in Parliament*, London, 1962.

Mitchell, David, *Queen Christabel, A biography of Christabel Pankhurst*, London, 1977.

Oxford National Dictionary of Bibliography, online edition, www.oxforddnb. com, 2004 and updates.

Pankhurst, Christabel, Ed Lord Pethick-Lawrence, *Unshackled, the story of how we won the vote*, London, 1959.

Purvis, June, *Women's History: Britain, 1850-1945*, London, 1995, reprinted 1997 and 1998.

Purvis, June, *Emmeline Pankhurst, a biography*, London, 2002.

Rosen, Andrew, *Rise Up Women! The Militant Campaign of the Women's Social and Political Union 1903-1914*, London, 1974.

Rover, Constance, *Women's Suffrage and British Politics*, London, 1967.

Russell, A.K., *The Liberal Landslide, The General Election of 1906,* Newton Abbot, 1973.

Smith, Harold H., *The British Women's Suffrage Campaign 1866-1928*, Harlow, 1998, revised second edition, 2010.

The Times Guide to the House of Commons 1910, London, 1910, Reprinted 2004.

The Times Guide to the House of Commons 1911, London 1911, Reprinted 2004.

The Times Guide to the House of Commons 1919, London, 1919, Reprinted 2004.

Threlfall, Richard, *The story of 100 years of phosphorus making 1851-1951*, Oldbury, 1951.

Wingerden, Sophia A. van, *The Women's Suffrage Movement in Britain, 1866-1928*, Basingstoke, 1999.

Appendix One
The Seventeen Pioneers

There were seventeen women candidates in 1918. Only one was elected, Mme Markievicz for the Sinn Fein in Dublin St. Patrick's, but she chose to sit in the *Dáil Éireann*. None of the original seventeen pioneer candidates were to be elected to the House of Commons. Five women stood as independents, four for Labour, four for the Liberals, two for Sinn Fein, and one each for the Unionists and the Women's Party. The youngest was aged 31 in 1918, the eldest aged 74. The House of Commons had 707 seats and a registered electorate of 21,371,612 with 10,761,705 casting a vote. Women candidates secured 58,978 votes.

Each of the seventeen women were remarkable by any criteria. Two, McEwan (Enfield) and Lucas (Kennington) had stood in for their husbands, the latter just a fortnight after he had died. Five had strong connections to Ireland and its politics: Markievicz (Dublin, St Patricks), Carney (Belfast, Victoria), Despard (Battersea North), Dacre Fox (Richmond), Pethick-Lawrence (Manchester, Rusholme). Several had had brushes with the law: Markievicz had been sentenced to death for her part in the Easter uprising, reprieved and was in prison during the election, Carney spent eight months in prison for her part in the Easter uprising, Despard was imprisoned for her suffragette activities, Pethick-Lawrence suffered force feeding in Holloway prison, Murray

(Glasgow, Bridgetown) and Dacre Fox had both been arrested whilst campaigning in London, Pankhurst (Smethwick) had fled into exile. Dacre Fox was to be interned as a fascist during the Second World War. Several of them had fallen out with Emmeline Pankhurst.

The results quoted here are taken from *The Times Guide to the House of Commons 1919,* London. The potted biographies are just that, an outline of some remarkable people who led remarkable lives, both before and, in some cases, after the 1918 General Election.

Key: *Ind. = Independent; Lab. = Labour; L. = Liberal; U. = Unionist; S.F. = Sinn Fein; W.P. = Women's Party; Co.N.D.P. = Coalition National Democratic Party; N. = Irish Nationalists; Co. = Coalition. *= lost deposit.*

Mrs. Margery Corbett Ashby   Birmingham, Ladywood
1882-1981. Age in 1918: 36

Margery Corbett Ashby **(see chapter 4)** was to fight seven Parliamentary elections as a Liberal candidate. Her failure to get elected didn't prevent her playing a very full part in public life both in the UK and further afield. Her father and mother were both Liberal activists. She was educated at home and went to Newnham College, Cambridge where she was active in the Political Society, and in various suffragist groups. Shortly after graduation she played a major part in her father's successful election campaign to serve one term in the 1906 Parliament.

She was a founder member of the International Women's Alliance and in 1920 became honorary president. Her ability to speak languages enabled her to converse in Turkish to President Kemal Ataturk and calm down a difficult meeting in Rome with a speech in Italian. Following her first election she was asked by the British to start a women's police service, first in Cologne and later for the whole of Germany. During the Second World War she went to Sweden and managed anti-Nazi propaganda.

One of her enduring legacies was to be co-founder of the Townswomen's Guild. She married a barrister, Arthur Ashby, in 1910 and had one son. She was made a Dame Commander of the British Empire (DBE) in 1967. In 1978 she attended the opening of an exhibition in Westminster Hall to celebrate the 50th anniversary of women having the vote on the same basis as men.[181]

Electorate: 33,330. Turnout 40.6%

Candidates	Party	Votes	Percentage
A.N. Chamberlain	U	9406	69.5
J.W. Kneeshaw	Lab	2572	19.0
Mrs. M.I. Corbett Ashby	L	*1552	11.5
Majority		6833	50.5%

Miss Winifred Carney   Belfast, Victoria

1887-1943. Age in 1918: 31

Winifred Carney was the youngest woman to contest the 1918 General Election. She was born in Bangor, County Down and attended a Catholic school. After qualifying as a secretary, she became active in suffragist and socialist politics eventually becoming secretary of the Textile Workers Union in Belfast. She was very close to James Connolly who asked her to join him in the Dublin Post Office during the 1916 Easter insurrection. She stayed for the duration of the siege and spent eight months in prison.

After 1918 she continued working for the Irish Transport and General Workers Union, married a Welshman who was believed to be an Orangeman, and continued in left wing politics.[182]

---

181 'Obituary: Dame Margery Corbett Ashby, A life devoted to work for the emancipation of women', *The Times*, 16 May 1981; Simkin, J., 'Margery Corbett Ashby' *Spartacus Educational* http://spartacus-educational.com/Washby.htm, 1997, updated 2014, downloaded 15 September 2017; 'Dame Margery Corbett Ashby', *Encyclopaedia Britannica Online*, https://www.britannica.com/biography/Margery-Corbett-Ashby, downloaded 15 September 2017.

182 "Winifred Carney", *Dictionary of Ulster Biography* , http://www.newulsterbiography. co.uk/index.php/home/viewPerson/225, undated, downloaded 13 September 2017; "Winifred Carney, A typewriter and a gun" *BBC Voices*, http://www.bbc.co.uk/ programmes/articles/19ytB8NQdgzxg95sDMdDhb2/winifred-carney, undated, downloaded 15 September 2017.

Electorate: not available. Turnout: not available

Candidates	Party	Votes	%
T. Donald	Lab U	9309	70.7
R. Waugh	Lab	3469	26.3
Miss M. Carney	S.F.	*395	3.0
Majority		5840	44.4

Mrs. Charlotte Despard   Battersea, North

1844-1939. Age in 1918: 74

At 74 Charlotte Despard was the oldest woman to stand as a candidate in 1918. She was the eldest daughter of a naval commander, J. T. W. French. Her younger brother became Field Marshall Sir John French who led British Forces in France during the First World War. Charlotte played a large part in his upbringing as both of their parents were dead by the time she was nine. It was a major cause of pain for her that their divergent political views were to estrange them in later life, especially when he was Lord Lieutenant of Ireland from 1918 to 1921 when she was openly working with Sinn Fein.

She married the wealthy and liberal Maximilian Despard in 1870. Over the next twenty years she wrote novels until her husband died in 1890. After a year as a Poor Law Guardian she decided to move to Nine Elms in London and began to work among poor people, opening one of the first child welfare centres and setting up working men's clubs. She joined the Independent Labour Party because she considered it better understood the position of women whose equality was a condition of complete democracy. Her striving for democracy led her to break with the Pankhurst-led Women's Political and Social Union to set up the Women's Freedom League. She refused to pay taxes, took part in many "scenes" and spent time in prison. On the outbreak of war, she threw herself into the peace movement.

After the 1918 election Charlotte went to live in Dublin and gave her strong support to de Valera, both before the treaty and afterwards, which brought her into conflict with the authorities. She returned to suffrage issues in 1926 when, at the age of 82, she marched through London supporting the demand for women's franchise on the same basis as men. In 1930 she travelled to Russia and on her return to Dublin she set up a college for the political education of workers. During anti-communist riots in 1933 the premises were besieged and stoned, with Charlotte inside.[183]

Electorate: 38552. Turnout: 43.7%

Candidates	Party	Votes	%
R. Morris	Co. U.	11231	66.6
Mrs. C. Despard	Lab	5634	33.4
Majority		5597	33.2

Mrs. Norah Dacre Fox   Richmond

1878-1961. Age in 1918: 40

Norah Dacre Fox had been brought up in nearby Teddington, to where her Protestant family had moved from Ireland. She married Charles Dacre Fox in 1909. In 1912 she joined the militant Women's Social and Political Union and quickly rose through its ranks. She was involved in a number of incidents and arrested several times, most notably at Buckingham Palace when she attempted to deliver a letter from Emmeline Pankhurst to the King. When war broke out she joined the WSPU's campaign to support the war effort. By 1918 she was organising mass rallies calling for the internment of every enemy alien.

She chose to stand as an independent candidate in 1918. Her politics then gradually moved to the right. In 1922 she had a child and styled herself Norah Elam. She became an enthusiastic member

---

183 'Mrs Despard, Suffragist Leader and Social Worker', *The Times*, 11 November 1939; Simkin, J., 'Charlotte Despard', *Spartacus Educational* http://spartacus-educational. com/Wdespard.htm, 1997 updated 2015, downloaded 12 September 2017. **Further reading:** Linklater, Andro, *An unhusbanded life : Charlotte Despard, suffragette, socialist and Sinn Feiner*, London, 1980; Mulvihill, Margaret, *Charlotte Despard: a biography*, London, 1989.

of the British Union of Fascists and was among the first to be interned under the 18B defence regulations in 1940. She broke with Mosley after her release.[184]

Electorate: 32900. Turnout: 53.8%

Candidates	Party	Votes	%
C.B. Edgar	Co.C	8364	47.4
Mrs. N.D. Fox	Ind	3615	20.4
R.J. Morrison	L	3491	19.7
W.W. Crotch	Ind	2220	12.5
Majority		4749	12.5

Miss Alison Vickers Garland   Portsmouth, South

1862-1939. Age in 1918: 56

Alison Garland was the daughter of a silversmith from Liverpool who had married his dead wife's sister, at that time an unlawful and clandestine marriage, whilst both were living at an inn in London, with Alison's elder sister being born soon after. This unusual family arrangement may have encouraged Alison Garland to have a radical view of politics. She was heavily involved with both the Liberal Party and the suffragist movement, working within the Liberal Party over many years to persuade the party to adopt women's suffrage. In her late thirties, she was able to attend the Indian National Congress in Lucknow. She took the opportunity to travel and collected money for famine relief, work she continued on her return to the UK.

Eventually elected to the executive of the Women's National Liberal Federation, she made repeated attempts at the highest levels to get a settlement within the Liberal Party, especially when they were able to form a government. Some credit her with the authorship of a play called

---

184 'Three militants arrested at Buckingham Palace', *The Times*, 31 July 1914; 'Enemy Aliens', *The Times*, 30 July 1918; 'Leading Fascists Arrested, Sir O Mosley and eight others detained', *The Times*, 24 May 1940.

Simkin, J 'Norah Dacre Fox (Norah Elam)', *Spartacus Educational* http://spartacus-educational.com/Wdacrefox.htm, 1997 undated 2015, downloaded 13 September 2017.

The Better Half, which depicted a world in which only women could vote and men were demanding the suffrage.

After the 1918 election, she tried to enter Parliament at elections in 1922 and 1929. She continued her work with the Liberal Party, eventually becoming president of the Women's National Liberal Federation. She was awarded an OBE in 1937. She never married.[185]

Electorate: 37427. Turnout: 62.0%

Candidates	Party	Votes	%
H.R. Cayzer	Co.C	15842	68.3
Miss A.V. Garland	L	4283	18.5
J. Lacey	Lab	3070	13.2
Majority		11559	49.8

Mrs. Emmeline Pethick-Lawrence   Manchester, Rusholme

1867-1954. Age in 1918: 51

Emmeline Pethick was the daughter of a Methodist businessman in Bristol and educated at a Quaker boarding school, where she was often in trouble. In her mid-twenties she became a volunteer social worker at the West London Methodist Mission. In 1899 she met a wealthy lawyer Frederick Lawrence, they married in 1901 and agreed to have the joint surname of Pethick-Lawrence.

Frederick's wealth and legal expertise and Emmeline's organisational skills were important to the growing suffrage movement which they joined in 1905, after being introduced to the Pankhursts by Keir Hardie. Emmeline believed in the evolution of women and combined flowery language with a careful eye on suffragette funds. She is credited with having introduced the symbolic suffragette colours of purple, white and green and organising annual fundraising rallies for the Women's Political and Social Union at the Royal Albert Hall. She co-edited with

---

185 Coronation Honours, *The Times,* 12 May 1937; Crawford, E., *The Women's Suffrage Movement: a reference guide 1866-1928,* London, 1999; Mark Pottle, "Garland, Alison Vickers", *Oxford Dictionary of National Biography,* 2004; email from G. Hartley 2 November 2017.

Christabel Pankhurst the newspaper *Votes for Women*. In 1906 she went to prison for the first time, and then on four subsequent occasions. In 1912 she suffered force-feeding at Holloway prison. Soon after she and Lawrence were charged with conspiracy and suffered financially.

However, the Pankhursts, decided to take a more extreme approach which the Pethick-Lawrences questioned. The outcome was that they were effectively pushed out of the WSPU, focusing on the non-violent United Suffragists. After the war, she was involved in many campaigns such as British policy in Ireland for economic equality between the sexes. Meanwhile, her husband's political career flourished, with him becoming a Member of Parliament and eventually a member of the House of Lords. During the 1930s she became increasingly deaf and suffered other disabilities, but found time to write her autobiography. The Pethick-Lawrences had no children.[186]

Electorate: 30421. Turnout: 62.9%.

Candidates	Party	Votes	%
R.B. Stoker+	Co.C.	12447	65.1
W. Butterworth	L	3699	19.3
Mrs. E.P. Pethick-Lawrence	Lab	2985	15.6
Majority		8748	45.8

Mrs. Alice Lucas   Lambeth, Kennington

1853-1924. Age in 1918: 65

When nominations closed for the 1918 General Election there had been just sixteen women nominated as candidates. Mrs. Alice Lucas was the wife of the Unionist candidate and former Member of Parliament for Kennington, Colonel Francis A. Lucas. She had no intention of becoming the first Jewish woman to stand for Parliament.

---

186 Raeburn, A., 'Widening the Battle', *The Times*, London 030268. Harrison, B., "Lawrence, Emmeline Pethick-, Lady Pethick-Lawrence", *Oxford Dictionary of National Biography*, 2004; Simkin, J., 'Emmeline Pethick-Lawrence', *Spartacus Educational* website, 1997 undated 2015, http://spartacus-educational.com/Wpethick.htm downloaded 1 September 2017.

Colonel Lucas had previously been MP for Lowestoft between 1900 and 1906 and had contested Kennington in both 1910 elections. However, on 11 December after nominations had closed, he suffered a heart attack and died. The agreement of the Unionist Party leadership to give the "Coupon" to his sitting Liberal opponent may have contributed to Mrs Lucas's immediate decision to stand in his place. A close family friend, Sir John Hart Dunne, by then Britain's only surviving Crimean General, certainly thought so, and even suggested his treatment by the Unionists may have accelerated Lucas's sudden death.

Alice Lucas was born in 1853, the daughter of Viscount de Stern and sister of Sydney Stern, a Tory MP, later Lord Wandsworth. Polling was delayed until Christmas Eve less than a fortnight after Colonel Lucas's death. *The Times* reported that it was a very subdued election. Alice Lucas died in May 1924, aged 69.[187]

Electorate: 37322. Turnout: 29.7%**

Candidates	Party	Votes	%
H.G. Purchase+	Co.L	4705	42.4
Mrs. A. Lucas	C	3573	32.2
W. Glennie	Lab	2817	25.4
Majority		1132	10.2

**This poll was delayed until 24 December 1918.

Lucas described as U in Times, but C in Craig

Miss Mary Macarthur (Mrs W.C. Anderson)   **Stourbridge, Worcs**
1880-1921. Age in 1918: 38

Mary Macarthur **(see chapter 3)** was the daughter of a draper from Glasgow. Educated locally, she studied for a short period in Germany. *The Times* described her as "one of the most striking personalities in the Labour movement". It was also revealed that she had declined the offer

187 'News in Brief', *The Times*, 20 December 1918; 'The Kennington Contest', *The Times*, 18 December 1918; 'Mrs Alice Lucas', *The Times*, 9 May 1922; Email G. Hartley 9 September 2017.

of the award of the DBE. Days before she died she had a telephone – then a very new piece of technology – installed by her bedside to enable her to continue working with the National Federation of Women's Workers, which at that time was in the process of amalgamating with the mixed sex General and Municipal Workers' Union. Initially she had adopted her father's conservative views, but she attended a meeting to discuss setting up a local branch of the shop workers' union and was won over to trade unionism and later to socialism.

She rapidly moved up the trades union movement with a notable reputation for supporting the rights of sweated female labour. Initially she encouraged women to join male trades union, and to get male trade unionists to welcome women members.

In 1906 she established the NFWW and edited the weekly *Woman Worker* newspaper. She joined the executive of the Independent Labour Party and met her husband William Anderson, by whom she had a daughter. Anderson became Member of Parliament for Attercliffe, though he lost his seat in the 1918 General Election and died soon after. Mary was a passionate supporter of universal adult suffrage rather than specifically women's suffrage. During the First World War she worked to mobilise women workers for the war effort.

After the 1918 General Election and the death of her husband she continued her trades union work but in 1920 was diagnosed with cancer and died on New Year's Day 1921.[188]

Electorate: 42206. Turnout: 55.0%

Candidates	Party	Votes	%
Rt. Hon. J.W. Wilson +	L	8920	38.5
Miss M.R. Macarthur	Lab	7587	32.7
F.V. Fisher	Co.NDP	6690	28.8
Majority		1,333	5.8

---

188 'Death of Mary Macarthur, Champion of Women Workers', *The Times*, 3 January 1921; John, A.V., 'Macarthur [married name Anderson], Mary Reid', Oxford Dictionary of National Biography, 2004, https://doi.org/10.1093/ref:odnb/30411, downloaded 3 March 2018.

Miss Violet Markham, (Mrs Carruthers)   **Mansfield, Notts**

1872-1959. Age in 1918: 46

Violet Markham actively campaigned against women having the vote and often spoke at anti-suffrage demonstrations organised by Lords Curzon and Cromer and other male anti-suffragists. In 1918, once women had won the right to vote, she decided to stand as a candidate. She later played a very full part in public life and, remarkably for that time, continued to use her maiden name, despite having married Lieutenant-Colonel James Carruthers in 1915. Her father was the part-owner of Markham Colliery, then one of the most up-to-date and productive mines in the country. Her grandfather on her mother's side designed the Great Exhibition and Crystal Palace. Her interest in industry led to her being appointed to the Central Committee of Women's Training and Employment in 1914 and thereafter she was on many other committees connected with industry and training. She was a longstanding member of Chesterfield town council, chairing the education committee and serving as mayor in 1927. In 1921 she accompanied her husband to Cologne where he was part of the army of occupation. She also travelled widely abroad, especially to South Africa. She wrote and published extensively, mainly about her time in Germany and South Africa.[189]

Electorate: 39041. Turnout: 52.5%

Candidates	Party	Votes	%
W. Carter	Lab	8957	43.6
G.W.S. Jarrett	Co NDP	6878	32.6
Miss V. Markham	Ind L	4000	19.5
Dr. N.M. Tranchard	Ind	*878	4.3
Majority		2279	11.0

---

189 'Obituary: Miss Violet Markham, in the forefront of public life', *The Times*, 3 February 1959; Jones, H.,'Markham, Violet Rosa', *Oxford Dictionary of National Biography*, 2004; 'Markham, Violet Rosa, 1872-1959, liberal activist and public servant', *AIM 25 Archives in London and the M25 area*, http://www.aim25.com/cgi-bin/vcdf/detail?coll_id=5642&inst_id=1&nv1=search&nv2, downloaded 12 September 2017.

Mrs. Edith How Martyn   **Hendon, Middx**

1875-1954. Age in 1918: 43

Edith How was the daughter of a grocer from Kent. She married Herbert Martyn in 1899. She studied at University College, Aberystwyth, and was awarded a BSc external degree from the University of London in 1903. She was the first woman associate of the Royal College of Science. She was the honorary secretary for the Women's Social and Political Union and one of the first suffragettes to go to prison in 1906. She was, however, disillusioned by Emmeline Pankhurst's autocratic leadership and left with others to establish the Women's Freedom League.

Apart from female suffrage, her other great interest was birth control and much of her life from 1910 was directed towards promoting it, both at home and abroad. In 1928 she set up the Suffragette Fellowship which did much to curate the memories of those involved in the pre-war campaigns.

Her unsuccessful campaign in 1918 was followed in 1919 by election as the first woman member of the Middlesex County Council. During the Second World War, she and her husband went to New Zealand and Australia where they settled.[190]

Electorate: 33117. Turnout: 59.4%

Candidates	Party	Votes	Percentage
P. Lloyd-Graeme	Co.C	14431	73.4
F. Bailey	Lab	3159	16.1
Mrs. E.H. Martyn	Ind. Prog	*2067	10.5
Majority		11272	57.3

190 "Obituary, Edith How Martyn", *The Times*, 4 February 1954; Frances, Hilary, "Martyn, Edith How", *Oxford Dictionary of National Biography*, 2004; Simkin, J., "Edith How-Martyn", *Spartacus Educational*, 1997 updated 2015, http://spartacus-educational.com/Wmartyn.htm downloaded 1 September 2017.

Mrs. Janet McEwan   **Enfield, Middx**

1860-1921. Age in 1918: 58

Janet McEwan's husband, John, had been selected as the prospective Liberal candidate for Enfield five years before in anticipation of a General Election in 1914 or 1915. However ill health forced him to retire from his business activities in the tea and rubber industries and as the prospective candidate. Janet was unanimously selected as her husband's successor. Both were heavily involved in the local community and Presbyterian Church.

John was the Chair of Governors at Birkbeck College, London. Janet Chaired the Enfield Maternity Centre and was on the local education and juvenile advisory committees.

During the war, Enfield's population had been swelled by migrant munitions workers from the north, which created enormous housing problems but also provided a boost to the Labour vote. She came third, losing her deposit behind the Coalition Conservative who had previously represented the seat for sixteen years until defeated in 1906, and the Labour candidate who was the assistant secretary of the Railway Clerks Association. Janet fell ill in 1920 and died in February 1921.[191]

Electorate:30031. Turnout: 54.8%

Candidates	Party	Votes	%
H.F. Bowles	Co.C	8290	50.4
W.E. Hill	Lab	6176	37.5
Mrs. J.L. McEwan	L	*1987	12.1
Majority		2114	12.9

191 'Obituary Mrs J McEwan', *Enfield Gazette*, 20 February, 1920; 'Death of Mr John McEwan', *Enfield Weekly Herald*, 14 March 1924; 'Three Cornered Fight at Enfield, Mrs McEwan's candidature', *The Times*, 13 December 1918.

Mrs. Millicent Mackenzie   **University of Wales**

1863-1942. Age in 1918: 55

In 1904 Hester Millicent Mackenzie, always known as Millicent, was appointed the first woman professor in Britain and the first female member of the University of Cardiff senate. She was the daughter of William Hughes of Bristol and married Professor John Stuart Mackenzie in 1898. She was a well-known educator, publishing several books and was a leading advocate of training women to teach. Her most important book, *Hegel's Educational Theory and Practice*, was published in 1909. She was a leading suffragette and set up a branch of the Women's Suffrage Society in Cardiff. Both she and her husband retired from the University in 1915 to travel and write. She took a keen interest in the work of the educational philosopher, Rudolf Steiner, and organised conferences and tours to promote his work.[192]

Electorate: 1066. Turnout: 85.8%

Candidates	Party	Votes	%
Rt. Hon. J.H. Lewis	Co.L	739	80.8
Mrs. H.M. Mackenzie	Lab	176	19.2
Majority		563	61.6

Mme. Constance Markievicz   **Dublin, St. Pancras**

1868-1927. Age in 1918: 50

Constance Gore-Booth was born into a landed Anglo-Irish family with a seat at Lissadell, County Sligo. Constance had been presented to Queen Victoria at court but soon after went to study painting in Paris where she met and later married, in 1900, Casimer Markievicz, a Polish count. The couple moved to Dublin where they mixed in the city's artistic circles.

---

192 Page,K., 'First female professor appointed in the biggest coal port in the world', *We Are Cardiff Blog*, https://wearecardiff.co.uk/2013/03/08/international-womens-day-a-guest-post-by-kelly-page/ 2013, downloaded 14 September 2017; 'The UK's first female professor: Millicent Mackenzie', *Cardiff University Blogs: Archives and Record Management*, http://blogs.cardiff.ac.uk/cuarm/millicent-mackenzie/ , 2015, downloaded 15 September 2017.

She became increasingly interested in Irish nationalist politics, having already been committed to women's suffrage. She made a dramatic intervention in a 1908 Parliamentary by-election in Manchester by driving a four in hand wagon through the streets in support of the right of barmaids to serve behind bars, as part of a campaign against the anti-suffrage stance of the Liberal candidate, Winston Churchill.

During the First World War, Markievicz promoted Irish neutrality and made no secret of her support for armed rebellion. She took part in the 1916 uprising, was captured and sentenced to death, which was commuted to penal servitude for life because she was a woman. She was released as part of an amnesty in 1917 but then re-arrested in 1918. She was in prison when the 1918 General Election was called and subsequently won. On release in March 1919 she chose not to take her seat in the House of Commons but was appointed secretary for Labour in the *Dáil Éireann*. She served further prison terms and opposed the treaty which brought about the creation of the Irish Free State.[193]

Electorate: not available. Turnout: not available

Candidates	Party	Votes	Percentage
Markievicz, Mme.	SF	7835	65.8
W. Field +	N	3752	31.5
J.J. Kelly	Ind N	312	2.7
Majority		4083	34.3

193 Brookes, ibid, p11; Paseta, S, 'Markievicz [nee Gore-Booth], Constance Georgine, Countess Markievicz in the Polish nobility', *Oxford Dictionary of National Biography*, 2004 https://doi.org/10.1093/ref:odnb/37472, downloaded 20 March 1918.

Miss Eunice Murray   **Glasgow Bridgetown**

1877-1960. Age in 1918: 41

Eunice Murray was born in Cardoss, Dumbartonshire, and both her parents were American but lived in Port Glasgow. Her father was a lawyer, an abolitionist and a strong supporter of feminism, as was her mother who joined the Women's Freedom League with Eunice. By 1913 Murray had become President of the League in Scotland. In the same year, she attended the International Woman Suffrage Alliance conference in Budapest. She was one of four suffragettes who were arrested for speaking in Downing Street and on Horse Guards Parade. In fighting Glasgow Bridgetown, Eunice was taking on one of the most formidable leaders of the Labour movement, Jimmy Maxton, though the Coalition candidate won. In so doing, she became the first woman to contest a Scottish Parliamentary seat.

Eunice wrote extensively about the feminist movement, women, folklore, local history, and her mother. In 1923 she was elected to Dumbartonshire County Council. In 1945 she was awarded the MBE.[194]

Electorate: 37980. Turnout: 52.0%

Candidates	Party	Votes	%
A.M. Scott +	Co. L.	10887	55.2
J. Maxton	Lab	7860	39.8
Miss E.G. Murray	Ind	*991	5.0
Majority		3027	15.4

194 Leneman, L., 'Murray, Eunice Guthrie', *Oxford Dictionary of National Biography*, 2004, updated 2008; Fullarton, D., 'From suffragette to councillor', *Helensburg Heritage* website, updated 2018, http://www.helensburgh-heritage.co.uk/index.php?view= article&catid=39%3Apeople-&id=897%3Afrom-suffragette-to-councillor&tmpl= component&print=1&layout=default&page=&option=com_content&Itemid=399, downloaded 3 March 2018.

Miss Christabel Pankhurst   **Smethwick**

1880-1959. Age in 1918: 38

Christabel Pankhurst (**see chapter 2**) was born in Manchester. Her father was a lawyer. Her mother, Emmeline, was to become the most notable leader of the suffragette movement. When Christabel was six the family moved to London where her parents' home became a centre of political discussion and activity.

Whilst Christabel and her mother were in Geneva, shortly after her eighteenth birthday, her father died and the family were forced to move back to a smaller home in Manchester. She combined a job as a registrar and a shopkeeper whilst studying for a law degree at Manchester University.

Initially Christabel was a member of the Independent Labour Party but became increasingly critical. In 1903 her mother set up the Women's Social and Political Union to wage a more militant campaign for votes for women, with Christabel as a leading member. The WSPU campaign became increasingly violent.

By 1911, she had to flee to France for fear of arrest, where she continued to incite violence. The outbreak of war in 1914 brought a halt to the suffragette campaign, Christabel returned to London and undertook a propaganda campaign in aid of the war effort. When it became obvious that some women would be able to vote, the WSPU transformed itself into the Women's Party, with Christabel nominated as their prospective candidate.

Christabel stood in Smethwick but was defeated. There was talk of her contesting a by-election for the Westminster Abbey constituency but there was little support from her colleagues in the Women's Party so she was never nominated.

She subsequently became a Seventh Day Adventist and a writer on religion. She also began work on her own and her mother's biography. In 1936 she was awarded the DBE.

In 1939 she emigrated to California where she continued her religious work.[195]

Electorate: 32908. Turnout: 54.7%

Candidates	Party	Votes	%
J.E. Davison	Lab	9389	52.2
Miss C. Pankhurst	W.P.	8614	47.8
Majority		775	4.4

Miss Emily Phipps   Chelsea

1865-1943. Age in 1918: 53

Emily Phipps was born in Devonport, Devon. She went to Homerton College, Cambridge, and was awarded a first class honours degree in Latin and Greek from London University. In 1895 she moved to Swansea to take charge of a girls secondary school. She became a feminist after an incident at a meeting involving Lloyd George. She joined the Women's Freedom League. Three years later she led a protest against the census on the basis that if women didn't count for political purposes, they shouldn't count for statistical purposes. She and four colleagues spent census night in a cave.

During her election campaign in 1918 she encouraged women to vote by providing mock polling booths so that they would know what to do. She also arranged child care on the day of the election. Although describing herself as an "Independent Progressive", she was an active member of the Swansea Liberal Women's Association.

She was very active in the National Union of Teachers, playing a major part in the National Federation of Women's Teachers that worked within the NUT. She edited the NUWT's journal, *Woman Teacher*, and at

---

195 Purvis, J., 'Pankhurst, Dame Christabel Harriette', *Oxford Dictionary of National Biography*, 2004, updated 2011, https://doi.org/10.1093/ref:odnb/35375, downloaded 1 September 2017; Simpkin, J. 'Christabel Pankhurst', *Spartacus Educational* website, 1997, updated 2017, http://spartacus-educational.com/WpankhurstC.htm downloaded 1 September 2017.

one point campaigned for women to leave the NUT altogether and have their own union. In 1925, after studying in her fifties to be a barrister, she moved from Swansea to London. Swansea has honoured her memory by erecting a blue plaque in the city.[196]

Electorate: 24822. Turnout: 46.8%

Candidates	Party	Votes	%
Sir S.J.G. Hoare +	Co C	9159	79.1
Miss E.F. Phipps	Ind Prog	2419	20.9
Majority		6740	58.2

Mrs. Ray (Rachel) Strachey   Brentford and Chiswick, Middx

1887-1940. Age in 1918: 31

Rachel Costelloe, known as Ray, was born in Westminster, London. Her father was a solicitor and her mother a Quaker from Philadelphia who had eloped together. She graduated from Cambridge University in mathematics, attended lectures on electrical engineering at Oxford and spent a year studying abroad in Philadelphia. In 1911 she married Oliver Strachey, brother of the author Lytton Strachey, and spent a year in India. She became involved with the constitutionalist wing of the movement led by Millicent Fawcett in the National Union of Women's Suffrage Societies. She was actively involved in the Parliamentary lobbying which led to the 1918 extension of the franchise.

She stood for Parliament again in 1920 and 1922 and for some years acted as Parliamentary adviser to the first woman MP, Nancy Astor. At first this was unpaid, but later paid, alongside a salary from the Women's Employment Federation. She was a prolific writer on subjects ranging

---

196   Kean, H., 'Emily Phipps, Feminist and Headteacher', *Oxford Dictionary of National Biography*, 2003, updated 2008, https://doi.org/10.1093/ref:odnb/51782, downloaded 21 March 2018; *BBC* website 'Blue plaque for Swansea woman's campaigner Emily Phipps', http://www.bbc.co.uk/news/uk-wales-south-west-wales-24926599, 13 November 2013, downloaded 1 September 2017; *Women's Local Government Society* website, 'Suffrage Pioneers, Emily Phipps', http://www.suffrage-pioneers.net/the-list/emily-phipps/undated, downloaded 1 September 2017.

from India, some fiction, several biographies, including one of Millicent Fawcett, employment opportunities for women, and her best known work *The Cause,* which for many years was seen as the classic account of the women's movement in the UK.[197]

Electorate: 26409. Turnout: 49.1%

Candidates	Party	Votes	%
W.G. Morden	Co. C	9077	70.1
W. Haywood	Lab	2620	20.2
Mrs. R. Strachey	Ind	1263	9.7
Majority		6457	49.9

197 Caine, B., 'Strachey [nee Costelloe], Rachel Pearsall Conn [Ray]', *Oxford Dictionary of National Biography,* 2004, updated 2011, https://doi.org/10.1093/ref:odnb/38017, downloaded 1 September 2017; Simkin, J., Spartacus Educational, 'Ray Strachey', 1997, updated 2015, http://spartacus-educational.com/WstracheyR.htm, downloaded 1 September 2017.

Appendix 2
Election Manifestos

GENERAL ELECTION,
December 14th, 1918.

MISS
Christabel Pankhurst, Ll. B.,
Patriotic Candidate for Smethwick and
Supporter of the Coalition.

Printed by W. J. Durose, High Street, Smethwick, and Published by Elsie E. Bowerman, 355, High Street, Smethwick.

Election manifesto of Christabel Pankhurst.

MISS PANKHURST'S ELECTION ADDRESS.

To the Men and Women Electors of Smethwick.

OWING to the splendid patriotism and the generous chivalry to womanhood, shown by your honoured fellow-citizen, Major Thompson, and by his supporters, including those of his own family, there are only two candidates in the field in Smethwick.

I am standing as a Patriotic Candidate in the cause of a Victorious Peace and National and Imperial prosperity and advance.

I recognise that Mr. Lloyd George and the Coalition, have (by establishing unity of command, supplying munitions, and by other means) made it possible for our Soldiers and Sailors to win, by their heroism, the great victory over the Germans.

I also realise that the only possible alternative to the Coalition (headed by Mr. Lloyd George as Prime Minister, with Mr. Bonar Law at his right hand, and backed by the right sort of Labour men) would be a Government that would be a fatal danger to the nation, especially as regards the Peace settlement. Therefore I intend, if elected as member of Parliament for Smethwick, to give loyal support to Mr. Lloyd George, and the Coalition, in all their efforts to impose a Victorious Peace upon the enemy and to raise the Standard of Living of the people.

If elected to the House of Commons, I shall work for two main objects.

The first is a VICTORIOUS PEACE worthy of the Sacrifice which our Soldiers and Sailors have made—a Peace based on material guarantees against German aggression and not merely on German promises and scraps of paper.

The Germans must pay for the War and compensate their victims, but, as the Prime Minister has warned us, we must not let them do so by merely dumping cheap German goods on other countries. I maintain that the Germans must pay in the form of mineral deposits, and that they must forfeit to the Allies their mineral resources on this side of the Rhine. There could be no better guarantee of future peace, because Germany would thereby lose much of her warlike strength and would not dare to attack her neighbours in future.

Britain for the British must be the National Policy from now onwards, and the politics, finance commerce, and industry of this country must be defended against German penetration and intrigue. In particular, the enemy aliens who have been interned during the War, must be sent home to their own land, instead of being allowed to resume their dangerous activities here.

My second object is TRUE SOCIAL REFORM and especially INDUSTRIAL SALVATION. We must in future have not only Britain for the British, but a Britain worthy of the British. The Abolition of Poverty is an ideal which can and must be realised by means of increased Wealth Production, so that there may be enough to go round and provide the comforts and refinements of life for all. This in its turn means the provision of work for all willing workers. Indeed, my determination to work for the Abolition of Poverty, by increasing Wealth Production, and Democratising Prosperity, is one of my main reasons for seeking election to Parliament.

No programme of Social Reform is complete which does not guarantee the rights and the future welfare of the men of the Army and Navy who have risked everything for their country. Women, above all, understand and are grateful for the sacrifice of the Nation's Defenders and will show their gratitude in a practical way by their action at the Ballot Box and in the House of Commons.

As a Woman Member of Parliament, I shall, if elected, give special attention to the Housing Question, because, as every woman knows, a good home is the foundation of all well being. It is necessary that all New Housing Schemes shall help the woman in the home and relieve her burden of drudgery, by introducing bathrooms and various labour-saving arrangements, and also co-operation in the form of central hot water supply, central kitchens and laundries where these are desired by the householders concerned. Knowing that the right kind of Housing Reform is needed to ensure the health and comfort of parents and children and to protect the mother from overwork and make it easier for her to be a true companion to husband and children, I shall do my utmost to bring it about.

The welfare of the children is a foremost consideration with me. It is to defend the children's inheritance of freedom and to spare them the horrors of a future war that thousands of our brave men have given their lives in this war. Surely the rest of us should feel it a duty and privilege to save the children from bad social conditions, and to give them the chance of proper mental and bodily development.

A Good Education is the birthright of every child, and I shall do my utmost to give equal educational opportunities to all, and to improve the system of Education. This means, among other things, improving the position of the teachers, and thus enabling them to do even more for the children than at present.

By a Victorious Peace and by real Social Reform we shall preserve and strengthen the British Empire, which is the finest human organisation and the mightiest Champion of Freedom that the world has ever known.

Should the Men and Women Voters of Smethwick honour me by sending me to Parliament to represent them, I shall keep in close and constant touch with Smethwick. An Office will be opened in the Town, with a Local Secretary in charge, and I shall frequently visit and speak in the Constituency. When any difficulty arises which might prevent me from carrying into effect the principles and programme which you, as my constituents, and I, as your representative, believe in, I shall come to Smethwick to lay the facts of the case before you.

In conclusion, I should like to say once more how deeply touched I am by the action of Major Thompson and his Coalition Supporters, and to add that, if elected as Member for Smethwick, I shall do my best, by my action in the House of Commons, to be worthy of the sacrifice that has been made and of the trust that has been given to me by the people of Smethwick.

I am,

Yours faithfully,

CHRISTABEL PANKHURST.

WOMEN'S PARTY,
CENTRAL COMMITTEE ROOM,
112, HIGH STREET, SMETHWICK.

FELLOW CITIZENS

T the request of the STOURBRIDGE DIVISIONAL LABOUR PARTY, I have decided to stand as candidate for this Division at the forthcoming Parliamentary Election.

My candidature is endorsed by the National Labour Party, and has the warm support of the National Federation of Women Workers.

I STAND FOR THE AIMS and OBJECTS OF THE LABOUR PARTY, with whose comprehensive programme* you are doubtless familiar.

Its objects can be summarised as follows:—

TO UNITE ALL WHO CONTRIBUTE TO THE WEALTH AND WELFARE OF THE WORLD BY HAND OR BRAIN, TO SECURE, NOT PRIVILEGES FOR ANY SECTION OR CLASS OF THE COMMUNITY, BUT A FULL SHARE OF THE GOOD THINGS OF LIFE, MATERIAL AND SPIRITUAL, FOR ALL.

I DO NOT APOLOGISE FOR MY SEX. It takes a man and a woman to make THE IDEAL HOME, and I believe that neither can build THE IDEAL WORLD without the help of the other. In the new Parliament, where laws affecting every household in the land will be framed, the point of view of THE MOTHER, AS WELL AS THE FATHER, should find expression.

If I am returned to the House of Commons, I shall try to voice in a special sense the aspirations of THE WOMEN WORKERS OF THIS LAND, to whose cause I have been privileged to devote my life, and who, in every industrial centre in the United Kingdom and Ireland, are voluntarily contributing their pennies to the expenses of my Candidature.

I shall also feel entitled to speak for the WOMAN WHOSE WORK NEVER ENDS—the woman in the home, who faces and solves a multitude of problems every day—the woman who has been too often neglected or forgotten by politicians, the mother of the children upon whom THE FUTURE PRIDE AND STRENGTH OF THE NATION DEPENDS.

At the same time, I shall not be deflected from my duties to my constituents, men and women.

No legitimate grievance (individual or collective) which may be reported to me will remain unredressed, if it is humanly possible for me to get it rectified.

No reasonable request for any assistance within my power, as a Member of Parliament, and consistent with the Principles for which I stand, will be refused.

MY FOURTEEN POINTS

1.—A PEOPLE'S PERMANENT PEACE.

There must be NO MORE WAR, and the policy laid down by President Wilson seems to me most likely to achieve this aim. The Peace settlement must be based on Justice and Equity between the nations.

There must be an end of Secret Diplomacy I am opposed to the contemplated SITTING IN SECRET of the Peace Conference. Its meetings must take place in the FULL LIGHT OF DAY. THE VOICE OF LABOUR FROM ALL LANDS—and not only from the vanquished countries—must be heard, and its accredited representatives must have place at the Council Table of the Nations.

* It is fully expounded in a pamphlet entitled "Labour and the New Social Order" which can be obtained by any elector on application.

Election manifesto of Mary Macarthur.

2.—THE END OF CONSCRIPTION.

I will strive for the abolition, ROOT AND BRANCH, of Conscription, Military and Industrial, IN THIS AND ALL OTHER COUNTRIES.

3.—JUSTICE, NOT CHARITY, FOR SOLDIERS AND SAILORS.

All disabled men are entitled to AN ADEQUATE PENSION based on the cost of living. NO WIDOW OR CHILD SHOULD LACK THE NECESSITIES OF LIFE. Allowances to all dependents must be substantially raised, having regard to their needs and to the sacrifices made by the breadwinner for the country. THERE MUST BE NO SUGGESTION OF CHARITY.

4.—THE SPEEDY RETURN OF THE FIGHTING MEN.

Our soldiers and sailors want to get back to their homes and families. THEIR WIVES AND CHILDREN WANT THEM BACK. There must be no unnecessary delay. AMPLE ALLOWANCES MUST BE MADE FOR THE MEN AND THEIR FAMILIES until suitable work, at standard rates, is available.

5.—THE RESTORATION OF FREEDOM.

I will fight for Free Speech—a Free Press—Free Trial—for Social, Economic and Political Freedom—for the Repeal of D.O.R.A., and especially Clause 40D.

6.—A LIVING WAGE, AND NO UNEMPLOYMENT.

I hold that every worker is entitled to a wage sufficient to ensure not only the necessities, but the comforts of life. THE FEAR OF UNEMPLOYMENT MUST BE REMOVED once and for all, and suitable work provided for every willing worker.

7.—A MAN'S PAY FOR A MAN'S WORK.

It should be illegal to employ a woman on the same work as a man for less pay. The standard of life must not be lowered by unfair competition. THIS IS IN THE HIGHEST INTERESTS OF BOTH THE MEN AND THE WOMEN.

8.—THE REDEMPTION OF PLEDGES.

Promises made by the Government must be kept. They must not be regarded as mere scraps of paper, as in the past. Nothing has reflected more discredit on our Statesmen than their disregard of promises.

9.—A MILLION NEW HOMES.

The Housing Problems cannot wait. Local Authorities supported by grants in aid must be required to provide well-planned and healthy houses AT REASONABLE RENTS, with every labour-saving device, hot and cold water upstairs and downstairs, and plenty of cupboards. NO JERRY-BUILT DWELLINGS SHOULD BE TOLERATED.

RENTS MUST NOT BE UNFAIRLY INCREASED. The Rents Restriction Act should be extended for two years.

10.—SECURITY FOR ALLOTMENT HOLDERS.

The holders of allotments should be entitled to the full (fruits and vegetables!) of their labours, and must not arbitrarily be dispossessed of the land which they have cultivated. In this as in everything else private interest must make way for public good.

11.—THE GOLDEN KEY.

The best education must be within the reach of all. There should be NO DISTINCTION OF SEX, CLASS OR WEALTH FROM THE NURSERY SCHOOL TO THE UNIVERSITY. EVERY CHILD SHOULD HAVE AN EQUAL CHANCE. The financial problem for the parent must be solved by adequate maintenance grants. THE STATUS OF ALL TEACHERS, MEN AND WOMEN ALIKE, SHOULD BE RAISED. Their salaries, pensions and training should be on a scale commensurate with the honoured place which they ought to hold in the community.

12.—A FAIR SYSTEM OF TAXATION.

We shall have a war-debt of Seven Thousand Millions. Those who can best afford it must pay. I AM AGAINST ALL TAXES ON FOOD. The Income-Tax limit should be raised and further relief given in respect of family responsibilities. Super-Taxes and Death Duties should be increased. I am in favour of a Capital Levy exempting possessions under £1,000 and pressing lightly on possessions under £5,000.

13.—PUBLIC GOOD BEFORE PRIVATE PROFIT.

Land, Railways, Canals, Coal and Iron Mines, Life Assurance, Banking, Electricity and similar monopolies should be made public property, run FOR PUBLIC GOOD AND NOT FOR PRIVATE PROFIT. Equitable compensation should be given to existing owners and shareholders.

14.—THE DIGNITY OF LABOUR.

I believe in the Democratic Control of Industry. The workers should have a real share in management. Mere economic betterment is not enough. THEY ARE ENTITLED TO A FINER QUALITY AND TEXTURE OF LIFE, TO A NEW STATUS IN THE LAND.

I stand also for a MINISTRY OF HEALTH, the ABOLITION OF THE WORKHOUSE, INCREASED OLD AGE PENSIONS payable at 60, SELF-GOVERNMENT FOR IRELAND, COMPLETE ADULT SUFFRAGE, THE ABOLITION OF THE HOUSE OF LORDS, the ABOLITION OF THE PRESENT CORRUPT HONOURS SYSTEM.

With regard to Temperance, I shall loyally support the policy of the Labour Party, which is to TRUST THE PEOPLE, by enabling each locality to make its own conditions as to the sale and consumption or prohibition of drink within its own boundaries, in accordance with the desires of the majority of the people in the locality.

It finds the KEY TO TEMPERANCE REFORM in the taking of the manufacture and retailing of alcoholic drinks out of the hands of those who find personal profit in promoting the utmost possible consumption.

In this, as in all other social evils, I desire to get to the ROOT OF THE MATTER, and believe that the complete solution of this problem is bound up with the removal of bad social conditions generally.

THE ENGLAND WHICH SO MANY HAVE DIED FOR OUGHT TO BE WELL WORTH LIVING FOR. I desire to see it honoured among the nations for the Cleanliness and Beauty of its Cities, THE HAPPINESS AND HEALTH OF ITS CHILDREN, the Purity of its Politics and the Justice and Humanity of its Laws. I THEREFORE APPEAL TO THE ELECTORS OF THIS DIVISION, MEN AND WOMEN, TO SUPPORT THE IDEALS AND PURPOSE OF THE MOVEMENT WHOSE BANNER I AM PRIVILEGED TO CARRY.

Yours faithfully,

Mary R. Macarthur.

(Mrs. W. C. Anderson.)

CO-OPERATIVE ROOMS,
   STOURBRIDGE.
     28th November, 1918.

Printed by the Pelican Press (T.U.), 2 Carmelite Street, E.C., and published by Arthur Goddard, Election Agent, Market Street, Stourbridge.

Election manifesto of Margery Corbett Ashby, December 1918.

A SOLDIER'S WIFE FOR LADYWOOD.

CAPTAIN ASHBY

of the Queen's, who rejoined the Army when war broke out and is still in Belgium.

Printed and Published by the Templar Printing Works, Edmund Street, Birmingham.

TO THE ELECTORS OF LADY

A LEAGUE OF NATIONS: ~~including all nations~~

To make Another War Impossible.

~~To abolish Conscription.~~

To lighten the Burden of Taxation for Armaments.

To substitute Open Treaties ratified by Parliament for Secret Diplomacy.

To pool raw materials and food for the hungry peoples of the world.

Just as our common sense makes us agree to live together under a common rule of law and order within the nation, so I believe their common sense will teach the nations to live together in future, and I welcome the practical beginning of the idea in the International Council which will be established at the Peace Table to ration the nations.

FREE TRADE AND NO FOOD TAXES: We have made two outstanding contributions to the Allied cause:

By our unique Navy and Mercantile Marine we have secured the successful transport of troops, the feeding of our Allies, and the blockade of our enemies.

By our Free Trade wealth we have largely financed our Protectionist Allies.

The Premier's Preference proposals would make the ideal of a Free Breakfast Table impossible and curse the housewife's domestic budget with more profiteering.

RIGHTS OF LITTLE PEOPLES: Home Rule is imperative to give Ireland the same free choice of government we have demanded for Poland, Alsace-Lorraine, and Serbia.

HEALTH AND HOUSING: I believe the urgency of housing admits of no delay, and that there must be the immediate provision of

Houses with at least three bedrooms, bath-room, water laid on, within the average wage-earner's means.

A garden or allotment with each house, for those who want it.

State assistance to encourage municipal enterprise; the adequate taxation of land values; and the right of compulsory purchase of land for all public requirements at the rate-book valuation.

I regard the immediate provision of good labour-saving houses as one way of recognising the services of soldiers and workers at home and abroad and of helping to solve the evils of a low standard of health, temperance and morality.

A PROGRESSIVE PLATFORM

WOOD—WHAT I STAND FOR.

EQUAL CITIZENSHIP: Real equality between men and women before the law in

All questions of marriage, morals and the home.

Opportunities of general and technical training.

Equal pay for work of equal value above a sound minimum for all.

All trades, industries and professions.

LABOUR AND LEISURE:

A shorter working day and adequate minimum wage, enforced by law if necessary.

Adequate out-of-work Insurance.

More freedom and consultation in the workshop.

Public recreations of a who'esome kind.

SOLDIERS, SAILORS, AND MOTHERS: I believe in Justice without Charity to secure

Adequate pensions for widows with dependent children.

A real right of maintenance for wives.

Fullest possible help of all kinds to disabled or discharged soldiers and sailors.

Fair treatment for women war workers.

I welcome Mr. Asquith's desire to improve the Old Age Pensions secured by the Liberal Party, and should like to see the pension raised and the age limit lowered.

CIVIL AND INDUSTRIAL LIBERTY: I support the immediate restoration of

All British liberties of citizenship; and

All essential trade union rights for men and women to enjoy the full use of collective bargaining, surrendered or lost during the war.

TRADE AND TRANSIT: I favour

The removal of irksome Government control from private industries.

The encouragement of production by science, canals and railways.

The continued municipal ownership of electrical supply.

In general I should like to see more Municipal Administration and less Whitehall Bureaucracy.

Margery Corbett Ashby

FOR MEN AND WOMEN.

About the Author

DAVID Hallam signed up for the Master of Arts history course which led to this book just after his sixty-fifth birthday. He's delighted to have been designated an "MA" so late in life. His early academic life wasn't promising, but at the age of thirteen he began writing a regular column on cycle speedway for his local newspaper. By the skin of his teeth he got into Sussex University and was awarded a Bachelor of Arts in sociology. He later used the early skills gained from writing his local paper column to forge a career as a communications specialist. He made headline news many times. His greatest professional achievement was in the 1980s when he worked with a small charity and revealed the true extent of child sexual abuse across the UK. His interest in politics led him to serve as a councillor in Sandwell and then as a Member of the European Parliament, where he was known to be one of the most assiduous members. He is an enthusiastic Methodist. His first book *Eliza Asbury* (still in print) chronicles the life of Eliza Asbury the mother of Bishop Francis Asbury, the Methodist missionary to America. David doesn't like sitting still and has recently been elected to the National Members' Council of the Co-op Group, one of Britain's largest ethical retailers. After publishing *Taking on the Men*, he is looking for his next challenge.

Index